END YOUR SHYNESS & SOCIAL ANXIETY

The Adults' Guide & Workbook To Rebuild Your Social Skills And Restore Your Self-Belief In 3 Weeks Or Less

Copyright © 2024 by LearnWell Books.

All rights reserved. No part of this publication may be reproduced, distributed, or transmitted in any form or by any means, including photocopying, recording, or other electronic or mechanical methods, without the prior written permission of the publisher, except in the case of brief quotations embodied in critical reviews and certain other noncommercial uses permitted by copyright law.

References to historical events, real people, or real places are often fictitious. In such cases, the names, characters, and places are products of the author's imagination. We do this where it's important to protect the privacy of people, places, and things.

689 Burke Rd
Camberwell Victoria 3124
Australia

www.LearnWellBooks.com

We're led by God. Our business is also committed to supporting kids' charities. At the time of printing, we have donated well over $100,000 to enable mentoring services for underprivileged children. By choosing our books, you are helping children who desperately need it. Thank you.

This Is Really Important.
It's a Sincere Thank You.

My name is Wayne, the founder of LearnWell.

My Dad put a book in my hands when I was 13. It was written by Zig Ziglar and it changed the course of my life. Since then, it's been books that have helped me get over breakups, learn how to be a good friend, study the lives of good people and books have been the source of my persistence through some pretty challenging times.

My purpose is now to return the favor. To create books that might be the turning point in the lives of people around the world, just like they've been for me. It's enough to almost bring me to tears to think of you holding this book, seeking information and wisdom from something that I've helped to create. I'm moved in a way that I can't fully explain.

We're a small and 'beyond-enthusiastic' team here at LearnWell. We're writers, editors, researchers, designers, formatters (oh ... and a bookkeeper!) who take your decision to learn with us incredibly seriously. We consider it a privilege to be part of your learning journey. Thank you for allowing us to join you.

If there's anything we did really well, anything we messed up, or anything AT ALL that we could do better, would you please write to us and tell us (like, right now!) We would love to hear from you!

readers@learnwellbooks.com

We're sending you our thanks, our love and our very best wishes.

Wayne

and the team at LearnWell Books.

WELCOME TO OUR COMMUNITY

"It's like a private online book club"

 Imagine if you could actually meet and talk with other readers of this book and share your experiences.

 Imagine if you could chat with the author or join them on a live Q&A!

 Imagine getting access to the author's notes and other exclusive, unpublished material.

You can do all of that and a lot more in the LearnWell Online Community!!

→ Download your **Workbook**
→ Chat directly with the author!
→ Meet and feel supported by other readers and their experiences.
→ Access additional, exclusive content about this topic and others.
→ Join our live Author Q&A sessions online.
→ Learn faster, make lasting changes, and have 10 times more fun!

This is part of our commitment to creating the best learning resources in the world.

Scan the QR code to get FREE access
www.learnwellbooks.com/outgoing

To my younger self

Oh, the world that passed you by while you waited to feel good enough.

Never, ever make that mistake again.

You're enough.

You're loved.

Go do your thing!

CONTENTS

Introduction — 10

BOOK 1: HEALING TECHNIQUES — 15

1. **How It Feels** — 16
   The Real Truth About Living with Social Anxiety

2. **Why Do I Feel Like This** — 25
   Why People Struggle Socially

3. **Transform Your Thoughts Into Allies, Not Enemies** — 41
   Empowering Yourself For Social Interactions

4. **Turn Self-Doubt Into Self-Confidence** — 65
   Practices To Recognize Your Strengths & Celebrate Your Imperfections

5. **Relax!** — 84
   Your 5 Step Solution To Solve Fight Or Flight

BOOK 2: SOCIAL SKILLS — 101

1. **From Awkward To Awesome Through Better Communication** — 102
   The NASA Formula For Enhanced Social Confidence

2. **The Butterfly Emerges** — 123
   5 Strategies For Rapid Success

3	**From Fear To Fun With Gradual Exposure**	152
	Steps For Reclaiming Control Over Anxiety Triggers	
4	**Skip Over The Usual Social Hurdles**	178
	How Self-Compassion And Understanding Create Social Comfort	
5	**Staying On Track & Staying Social**	196
	How To Integrate This New Freedom Into Your Life, Forever	

Conclusion	212
References	214

YOUR
WORKBOOK

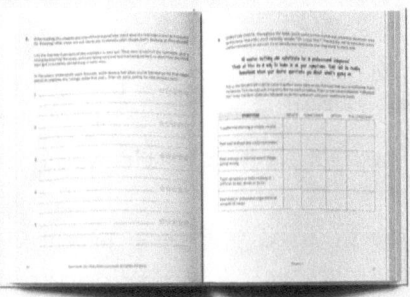

A shocking truth was discovered by a study done in 1987 – **people only remember 10% of what they read!**

That seems so discouraging.

But here's the **GOOD NEWS** – reading is **NEVER** a waste of time. As long as you do **one** important thing ...

The same study (by National Training Laboratories) shows that you will remember 90% of what you read when you **put your new knowledge into action**!

Here at LearnWell, we aim to create **the world's best learning resources**. So, we have included a highly engaging **Workbook** that helps you put your new knowledge into fun, practical action.

So, make sure you download your **FREE Workbook.** You'll find it located inside the **LearnWell Community.** Simply scan the QR code below for access.

Get your Workbook in the LearnWell Community
Scan the QR Code for access or go to:
www.learnwellbooks.com/outgoing

INTRODUCTION

Otters hold hands while they float down stream. Elephants cry when they lose a loved one. Dolphins call each other by name – even if it is in clicks and whistles. In a world where 2821 animal species rely on social connection to thrive, humans included, social anxiety is a silent form of torture.

These books are not here to tell you you're just shy and "need to get out more." They take what you're going through seriously.

I know you're here because you're searching for answers in a world that can make you feel like just about everyone has social anxiety so you might as well "get over it." Your search ends here. You've found a place where social anxiety is seen for what it really is – a connection killer. And from what we've already established, humans can't survive, let alone thrive without social connection.

I know what it's like to be the last one picked for a team sport. I know what it's like to miss your friends but cancel plans anyway. I know how it feels to isolate yourself so tightly that you forget what you're even running from. And, I know what it means to be lonely. I know you do, too.

You. Yes, you. In this moment right now. You're exactly where you need to be. These books are where you're finally safe. However, I can't promise that the journey you're about to embark on will be easy. The strategies and insights you will find may be confronting. Are you brave?

Maybe you don't think you are, but I'm asking you to trust that you have the guts to face this demon you're fighting. Even if you're not entirely sure what that demon looks like, or where to start, **just keep reading.**

In this book you will get to know a little bit more about me. Social anxiety is not the only battle I've conquered, but it is one that ruined my ability to connect with people for most of my life. It held me back in ways that rippled through my life and effected every other struggle I faced.

Along my healing journey, I often felt stunted and left behind by my peers. I felt small, insignificant, and lost. But once I searched for answers, like you're doing right now, things slowly fell into place. The ripples settled, and each effort I made to heal my social anxiety improved my other struggles as well.

Social anxiety is a struggle that lingered on long after I healed my depression and panic disorder. But as I sit, writing this book, it no longer has even a pinkies hold over me. It's gone. Vanished. And I couldn't be happier, or more confident in who I am. <u>I want nothing less for you.</u>

In a world with billions of other people, I knew I had to make a choice. Stay in my comfort zone, alone and full of fear? Or, face my fears and thrive? I think you can guess which one I chose. You're about to make the same choice.

This is where you're going to make the most important decision of this book. The choice to humor any sense of bravery you might have and read on. You need to be prepared to let go of what you think you know about social anxiety, and have an open mind to the proven strategies you're about to learn.

To build the best experience for you, I've created two books, each with 5 full chapters of lessons, insights, and exercises. You're going to play an active role in this process. These are not books for passive reading. They are books that will echo out into your real, everyday life – so long as you allow it.

Book one includes everything you need to know to start understanding and healing your social anxiety from the inside out. It includes the following insights:

- How to identify and understand social anxiety
- How your thoughts effect anxiety and what to do about it
- Why self-confidence really matters in this equation and how to get it
- Ways to cope with your social anxiety symptoms directly

This first book is about transforming your inner world into a place that is inhospitable for social anxiety to function. It's the first half of this book, but only a small fraction of the rest of your healing journey. However, without this first book, the methods and strategies in Book 2 will only scratch the surface of the issue.

Book two is where the real fun begins. This is the practical half of these two books, in the sense that it is where you will be ready to go out and start applying the things you learn in real life – with plenty of guidance, of course. It includes:

Introduction

- A plug-and-play strategy for building effortless connections
- Diving deeper into more advanced social strategies to make you unforgettable
- The most effective and exciting social anxiety strategy broken into steps you can take at any stage along your journey
- Insights into overcoming your biggest social fears
- A long-term game plan to keep making progress forever

The second book is the book of your journey where you will need courage. Nothing that's truly good every comes easy. You're going to have to fight your way through. However, I know how fear can cripple you. That's why I'm going to make you three promises.

Firstly: You don't have to let this process overwhelm you for it to work. This is not the time for jumping in the deep end. Every leap of faith you take will be calculated and controlled provided that you execute the action you take with self-care in mind.

My second promise to you is that at no point will I leave you in the dark. You will find prompts in most chapters that will encourage you to complete an exercise in your **Workbook**. I also suggest using the LearnWell Community. Please don't miss the opportunity to really immerse yourself in this recovery process.

And, my third promise to you is this: 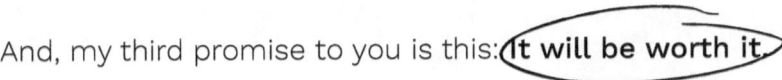 It will be worth it.

There is a whole life, a whole version of you waiting for you beyond these pages. You have the chance now to discover what being socially embraced, enjoyed, and cherished can feel like. Take the chance and find out.

Let these books be your window into the life you wish you had. But instead of having bars, the window is open and all your future friends are beckoning you from the other side. See that potential life for yourself as clearly as you can. It's possible and it's only 10 chapters away.

With these words, take my hand, and allow me to guide you on this incredibly personal, life-changing transformation. I'm here with you. Turn the page

BOOK 1

HEALING TECHNIQUES

1   **How It Feels**   16
       The Real Truth About Living with Social Anxiety

2   **Why Do I Feel Like This**   25
       Why People Struggle Socially

3   **Transform Your Thoughts Into Allies, Not Enemies**   41
       Empowering Yourself For Social Interactions

4   **Turn Self-Doubt Into Self-Confidence**   65
       Practices To Recognize Your Strengths & Celebrate Your Imperfections

5   **Relax!**   84
       Your 5 Step Solution To Solve Fight Or Flight

1

HOW IT FEELS

The Real Truth About Living with Social Anxiety

Hearing the navigational system of my phone say "Turn left" for the hundredth time, the tension in the car continued to grow. With a huff of frustration, my then-husband flicked on the indicator light.

"We should've been there by now." He growled. "Give me that thing!"

Grabbing my phone mid-left turn, he denounced my poor navigational skills. Defeated, I slumped in the passenger seat and looked at the passing city life. It was our first time driving in this city, and we'd taken the wrong turn onto the freeway.

Although the air was thick enough to cut with a knife, anticipating an argument with my husband was the least of my problems. My stomach churned, my palms were clammy, and my heart felt like it was pumping enough blood to fill an ocean. I was drowning in anxiety.

Deep down, a part of me secretly hoped that we were completely lost, or that our car could break down. We were on our way to his grandmother's nursing home for lunch but my body was reacting like it was about to be on the butcher's block.

"It can't get any worse than this." I thought. Then my husband's phone rang. As the ringtone broke the silence, we both looked down at the screen. It was his grandmother.

"Answer it." He said bluntly, "Tell her we're on our way."

Before I could begin to process the simple task he was asking me to do, I became frozen in fear. I began to plead with him to answer instead. I frantically told him that I'll put it on speaker phone and he can talk to her.

"Just answer it for God's sake, I'm concentrating!"

Still frozen, my body refused to move at all. Stuck in a moment of intense panic, I became consumed by the thoughts and fears fueling my now-racing heartbeat.

"What if I stumble over my words."

"What if I make a bad first impression before meeting her."

"What if she's angry that we're late for lunch."

"What if she thinks I'm stupid for getting mixed up with the directions."

What if. What if. What if … ?

Then, as the phone continued to ring, I thought about how embarrassing it would be to miss the call, and I began to imagine my husband telling his grandmother that it was **me** who didn't answer. So, although it was fear driving me, I began to fight.

I fought the immobilization keeping my arms fiercely locked to my chest. I fought my thoughts that were catastrophizing every possible outcome. I fought the urge to shout, "Stop the car!" to my frustrated, sleep-deprived husband. And I fought the sobs silently releasing from me with each breath. Defying every instinct within me, I picked up the phone and hit the green answer button.

Voice quivering, I answered with the most normal, "Hello." I could muster. Expecting my husband's grandmother to bite my head off on the call, I anxiously held the phone to my ear. To my surprise, the unfamiliar voice on the other side was soothing and sweet.

Kicking myself for being such an idiot, I listened to her say, "I'm right next to the gas station with the yellow pillars out front. No hurry, deary." I quickly hung up the phone with a final, "Okay, we're on our way." The conversation was quick, pleasant, and it had a positive outcome. The only thing wrong with the situation was the way I felt.

This is social anxiety.

THE CATALYST FOR MY RECOVERY

It wasn't the first time something like this had happened. Triggers for my social anxiety used to happen all the time. Dinner parties felt like danger zones. Grocery stores felt like a circus-show where I was the clown. And don't get me started on dealing with conflict. Every social interaction was layered with a nuance of fear, isolation, and self-loathing.

My fight-or-flight response has always been easily triggered by new and uncomfortable interactions with people. But what used to be normal awkward shyness quickly turned to social anxiety after losing my mother at the age of nine. My safety blanket felt as though it was torn away from me, and I was left bare to the scorching eyes and opinions of others. I could no longer hide behind her, gripping her skirt, as she navigated uncomfortable social interactions for me.

With the amount of mental health problems that ensued after this, it isn't such a shock that I ended up struggling with social anxiety too. But, when you consider that more than 12%[1] of the US population experiences social anxiety disorder at some point in their lives, you can see that it's not an uncommon condition.

However, I'm not writing this book to give you scientific definitions and statistics. I'm writing this book because I know you need relief. If you weren't struggling with social anxiety, you probably wouldn't be here right now. And that's why I need you to know that social anxiety in any form, even as a diagnosed disorder, is not a shackle and chains – at least not one without a key. You can overcome your social anxiety and become the social butterfly that you secretly are on the inside.

I know you don't avoid social events because you hate people. I know you fantasize about going to the grocery store without abandoning your cart or feeling like your soul is about to leave your body. I know that you want to go out without spending hours dressing because nothing in your closet is going to put a bandaid on your lack of self-confidence. I know all this, because <u>I used to be YOU.</u>

That day in the car with my now ex-husband wasn't just any other social anxiety attack. No, that day was the start of my recovery journey. It was the day that I saw a spark of strength within me that seemed too dim to exist before. I saw myself face one of my biggest fears - talking to a stranger on the phone. Although it was a small start to the mountain of challenges social anxiety brings, it was the catalyst to getting better and becoming who I am now.

I still had a very long way to go after hanging up the phone to my husband's grandmother. I still beat myself up for being "such a baby" about the situation. No one had ever explained social anxiety to me, so I just assumed that I was being an idiot and making a fool of myself for no good reason. Of course, this wasn't true and I was actually really struggling.

So, before we continue, I want you to know that it is NEVER your fault that you're struggling with social anxiety. However, it *is* entirely up to you to end your suffering. Don't worry about not knowing how, or where to begin. The truth is, you've already started. You're here.

EMBRACING SCARY THINGS

Once the call was over, I did feel a sense of relief and achievement for going through with it. I still felt angry with my husband for putting me in a position where I had to face the call or succumb to my anxiety. At the time, it was a big deal to me, and I still had to face the stress of meeting his grandmother and enduring a luncheon. Meeting your husband's grandmother for lunch doesn't sound too bad in theory, but social anxiety can ruin even the simplest social interactions.

However, despite the fear, the anxiety, and the amount of force it took for me to answer the phone, I wouldn't change a thing about that moment. I'm so glad that I felt cornered, with no way out besides doing the thing I didn't want to do. Because this was a moment that proved to me I CAN do scary things.

This moment showed me that there was bravery hidden behind my anxious exterior. Maybe I didn't realize the power of this moment right then and there, but the next time someone handed me the phone, you bet I answered it with 1% less hesitation than before. Sure, my heart race quickened, my palms felt clammy, and catastrophizing thoughts still spiraled around in my head. But I knew it was possible to push through the discomfort and answer the call anyway.

I'm not saying that you'll never feel anxious again by the end of these books. What I am saying is that after learning and practicing the methods beyond this first chapter, you will no longer let social anxiety rob you of your freedom. Social health is one of the core elements of a happy life. Living a happy life is why you're here and you deserve that. You deserve to be happy and I want that for you more than anything.

After years of practicing the methods I will teach you in these books, I see things differently than I did before. My anxiety has been replaced by a strong sense of curiosity. When my phone rings, the curiosity about who it is and what information I'm going to learn overpowers any anxiety I may have. I don't feel scared about potential negative outcomes. I know that I can handle whatever the call is about with confidence. I'm confident in myself and I genuinely don't care about what potentially negative things the person on the phone may think about me or if I sound awkward. I don't feel worried about messing up, stuttering, or forgetting what I wanted to say. I know that I'm human, and humans make mistakes.

These things apply to the many other social situations that used to cripple me in fear. After years of reshaping who I am, accepting the parts of myself that I didn't like before, and putting in the work to learn new ways to understand and manage my social anxiety, I can do things that once seemed impossible.

Not only can I speak on the phone with a total stranger, but I can eat at a restaurant without having an anxiety attack or leaving early. I can go to the grocery store and stay focused on what I need instead of becoming overwhelmed by the thought of all the eyes on me. I can say "yes" to dinner parties. I can take a video call with potential work clients without freezing up and thinking, "I'm not good enough." I can disappoint someone I love to stay true to myself. My fear of rejection or abandonment no longer controls me. I like who I am, and I CAN do things that scare me.

REPLACE FEAR WITH CURIOSITY

These books aren't about reshaping who you are into someone everybody likes. Not everyone will like you and that's okay. Remember that. However, these books *are* about becoming comfortable in any social setting without needing to be liked at all. It's about becoming so fearless that social settings become your playground rather than your prison.

I know you are a social butterfly hiding in a cocoon of self-doubt, negative thinking, and fear. But you must understand that you deserve the freedom and relief of spreading your wings and soaring through social challenges. You don't have to be trapped anymore. You can emerge, grow, and fly through life the way you've always dreamed of.

Social anxiety has made you feel inferior, but that's a trick. Maybe it's hard to believe sometimes, but I promise you, you have value. It will take work, and it will take guts, but it's time you rediscover that value so you can go out and confidently express it to the world.

You need to know that there is hope to live a life without this suffering. If you don't believe that, nothing's going to change. Having social anxiety does not make you weak. Just you being here, and wanting to **do** something about it proves you are strong. Let bravery be your backbone.

Facing this mountain is going to be scary at times. It will make you want to close this book and climb back into your bubble. But if you're willing to take the risk and replace fear with curiosity, I know that you're going to be so proud of yourself by the end of this. I'm already proud of you for getting this far. Now, all that's left to do is take another step forward.

To unlock yourself from the hold of social anxiety, you have to understand where it's coming from. It's not something that hits you out of the blue for no reason, even though it can feel like that sometimes. There is ALWAYS a reason.

So in this next chapter, we're going to uncloak the demon of social anxiety and shine a light on every facet of its ugly face. It's time you understand the truth: Everything your social anxiety has told you is false. You're stuck in its grip but there is a way out.

If you're ready to climb and claw your way to freedom and start living your life the way you deserve to, summon up a sense of curiosity and turn the page to chapter two. I know it's scary, but you CAN do scary things, and I'll be here to do them with you.

Before moving on, make sure you have the Workbook. It's an essential companion to this book. It will change your experience from hearing ideas to actually making powerful changes in your life. Go to: www.learnwellbooks.com/outgoing to get your free copy. Do that now, before you turn to the next chapter.

2

WHY DO I FEEL LIKE THIS

Why People Struggle Socially

"You're such a buzzkill."

The sting of the label was vinegar to a wound. My body was slightly hunched in an attempt to draw less attention to myself, I choked back tears as the words pulled me down.

I'd been invited to go out for the night and I knew what that meant: Swarms of people looking me up and down one after the other, drunk friends bumping into me shouting inaudible things across the busy dancefloor, and hours upon hours of social chit-chat. It was just too much.

Like a punch to the gut, the knot in my stomach arrived. Before I could say, "You know, I don't really feel like all that tonight." My face must've given it away. I'd been out with these friends a handful of times, but lately, it had become overwhelming.

I had stopped drinking alcohol for a few weeks, and I knew that it was the only crutch that allowed me to remotely enjoy myself socially. Without it, I was quiet, more reserved, and became easily overwhelmed. But I wasn't about to return to tequila shots and cocktails.

There was a good reason why I quit. Alcohol took the edge off the anxiety temporarily, but it had begun to backfire and cause severe anxiety the following day. I quit, but I watched my social life burn as a consequence.

This was the night my "friends" gave up on me. They'd had enough of me canceling almost every plan last minute or failing to enjoy myself while out. I had become the buzzkill of the group, and I was done for. Social anxiety had won.

It took me a long time to identify what I was going through. I didn't have a name for the feeling yet, but I knew something was wrong. I felt like I was failing, even though I had no control over the symptoms.

Growing up, I was labeled "shy" and "introverted." These labels made me feel like the symptoms were just a part of my identity. But, "buzzkill" transformed me into something else. It turned me into the source of others' unhappiness. I knew with that label that there was more to it all but it would still be years before I could name the experience and start improving.

Without knowing what was happening to me after every friendly wave or invite to lunch, things felt hopeless. Only once I understood that I had social anxiety and that there was something I could do about it my life changed forever. As scary as it was, I could pinpoint the problem and start working to resolve it.

You see, before you can overcome any fear, you have to understand it. I mean truly understand it. You need to know it back to front. You need to uncover it, decode it, and see it for what it *really* is. Once you are certain that social anxiety is the culprit, all that's left to do is know how to squash it. I need you to know that it's possible to do that. You can squash your social anxiety and be rid of it for good. But first, you need to identify it.

ARE YOU ANXIOUS, OR JUST SHY?

A quick determination you have to make before we continue is whether or not your symptoms are simply shyness or introversion.

Firstly, let's start with shyness. Shyness is a personality trait that is somewhat inherent in who you are. That means that you have the tendency to be more shy in social settings from a young age. You might be naturally soft-spoken, more inward in your appearance, and less outgoing.

Many factors can contribute to shyness, such as upbringing, genetics[2], social influence, or professional conditioning. Personality traits are largely related to environmental input but to some degree, everyone is born with natural traits and personalities. The bottom line is that shyness is a personality trait, like being talkative, adventurous, or compassionate.

Secondly, introversion has to do with your natural social battery. I'm sure you've heard about introverts and extroverts. Well, these are two of the "social types" that determine the amount of social interaction you can tolerate before becoming exhausted. The third social type is an ambivert, which is someone who finds themselves experiencing moments of introversion and times of extroversion.

> The differences between shyness and introversion are that shy people can be extroverted and introverts are not always shy. The two are not directly linked. Shyness lies in your demeanor and social presentation, whereas introversion is classified by having a shorter social battery.

The correlation between shyness, introversion, and social anxiety, is the similarities in how the three experiences present themselves to other people. One person can also show all three. The difference between the three experiences is how YOU feel rather than how you present yourself to others. So, to help you determine whether your current social experience is just an inherent trait or whether it is something more, I want to break social anxiety down for you.

THE ANATOMY OF SOCIAL ANXIETY

It's easier to identify what parts of your reaction to social situations are natural and what isn't if you can see the symptoms of anxiety laid out in front of you. Don't get me wrong, anxiety is a natural human response to danger. But that's exactly the problem, your body is experiencing a natural response to danger when you're completely safe.

Social anxiety is the body and mind going into fight-or-flight mode when there's no real danger. Fight-or-flight mode is your body's automatic protection mechanism that prepares you to either flee the situation or stay and fight. It's the switch that your brain flips to get your blood pumping and your senses sharper. Anxiety is when your brain flips the switch because of a thought or an emotion rather than a sign of physical danger.

I'm going to explain the connection between your mind, body, and emotions throughout this book, but for now, just know that when you feel anxious, you're experiencing what it would feel like to be chased down by a wild animal. The only difference is you get that feeling every time you talk to a stranger or sit around a dinner table. Your fight-or-flight response is triggered by the anticipation of a social interaction going wrong in some way, causing symptoms of anxiety.

Anxiety can be broken down into three sections of symptoms; Physical, behavioral, and cognitive.

Physical Anxiety Symptoms

Physical anxiety symptoms have everything to do with your body's fight-or-flight experience. Remember, it's preparing you to either run away from danger or freeze. While they are uncomfortable, they usually aren't dangerous. They include:

- Increased heart rate, palpitations, or pounding
- Sweating and clammy palms
- Blushing, or a sudden heat in the face and body
- Trembling or shaking
- Nausea or an upset stomach
- Lump in the throat
- Feeling light-headed or dizzy
- Shortness of breath
- Tense muscles

Behavioral Anxiety Symptoms

Behavioral symptoms are how you act while feeling anxious. They are the way you cope with your social anxiety. They can look like:

- Avoiding situations that put you at the center of attention.

- Avoiding activities where you might mess up or embarrass yourself.

- Overanalyzing interactions hours after they occurred.

- Canceling plans at the last minute out of fear or overwhelm.

- Excessive fidgeting or restlessness.

- Stuttering or stumbling over your words.

- A sudden need to avoid eye contact.

- Reliance on drugs or alcohol to cope.

- Shrinking your body posture to appear smaller.

- Becoming overly self-conscious.

Cognitive Anxiety Symptoms

Cognitive symptoms are your mind's reaction to anxiety. They are your thoughts and what happens to your thoughts while anxious. They include:

- An intense fear of being judged negatively.

- Worrying that others will notice your anxiety.

- Feeling anxious in anticipation of an event.

- Catastrophizing the outcome of an action or event.

- Repeating or saying negative things to yourself, i.e. negative self-talk.

- Debilitating fear of embarrassing yourself.

As uncomfortable as these symptoms can be, it's important for you to know that they are your body's way of protecting you from danger. They are simply your fight-or-flight responses in action. Once you know that, the logical way to cure anxiety is to remove yourself from the perceived danger or fight the perceived danger.

However, how you fight or flee from perceived danger is vital. If you don't do it correctly—using the methods throughout this book—you risk reinforcing that danger for yourself and making the problem worse. You risk getting caught up in the vicious cycle of anxiety, where your response to feeling anxious triggers more anxiety and leaves you anticipating the uncomfortable experience even after you feel better. This is also known as the Avoidance Cycle.

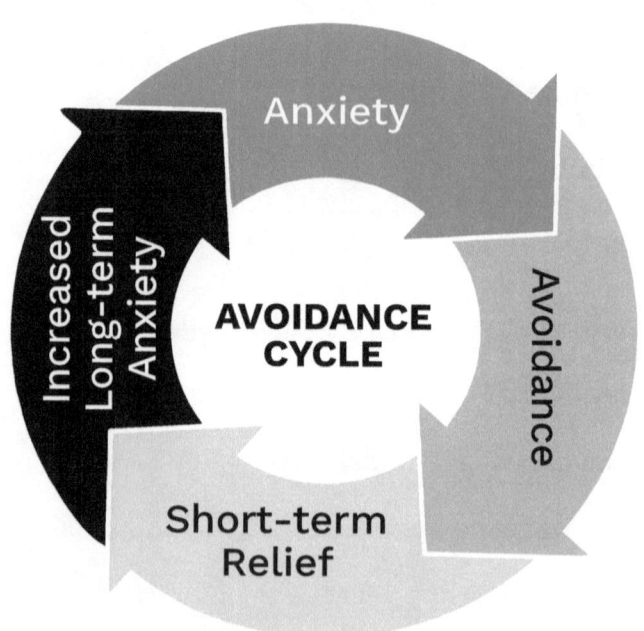

The Avoidance Cycle is when you feel anxious about an experience and you avoid it in an attempt to reduce the anxiety. The anxiety is instantly relieved as a result, but only for the short term. The next time you are faced with the same experience, the level of anticipation and anxiety is increased. And so the cycle continues.

I used to be caught in an avoidance cycle. I would be invited out to dinner, feel anxious about it, and use alcohol to avoid the situation. I would enjoy my night out for the most part, but once I woke up the next day, I hit a wall of panic, overwhelm, and exhaustion from socializing all night. Slowly, each time I was invited out, the anxiety got worse. Even once I stopped using alcohol to numb the anxiety, I simply replaced alcohol with physically avoiding going out at all.

The avoidance cycle not only made my social problem bigger but it caused me to lose my social life completely. Only when I could recognize that the culprit was social anxiety all along things got better.

It's natural to feel anxious occasionally, but if you reinforce the perceived danger for yourself by avoiding it in an unhealthy way, you are essentially proving to your mind and body that you are in real danger. That is why you must break the avoidance cycle, starting with knowing why you perceive danger in a social setting.

YOUR UNIQUE ANXIETY EXPERIENCE

I know sometimes it can feel scary even to remember what your anxiety feels like. But I want you to know that you are safe. That's something I need you to repeat to yourself over and over again throughout this book whenever things feel confronting. In fact, say it right now, out loud.

"I am safe."

Get used to the way it feels saying that.

"I am safe."

One more time, just for the heck of it.

"I am safe."

It might feel forced, but words have power and they can trigger thoughts and feelings. Chapter 3 is all about transforming your thoughts, so I'll leave that for later. But for now, I want you to start off your healing process with a bang. Keep this simple mantra in mind as we get into why you feel the way you do. This is where I want you to let go of what you believe anxiety is, and I want you to focus on what anxiety feels like for YOU. If you feel uneasy during this process, just remember, "I am safe," and push through.

The anxious mind can convince you that you are in danger, no matter how much you know you're not. The symptoms can sweep you off your feet and make you feel like you've lost control. The truth is, you probably have. Anxiety has claimed control over you in these moments, but that doesn't mean you can't get it back. You can remind yourself that you're okay and call your anxiety out for what it is: A false alarm!

If you have a preconceived idea of what is and what isn't anxiety, you might deny yourself the chance to reclaim your power. For

I AM SAFE

example, if your palms are sweating and you feel nauseous, but your friend with an anxiety disorder goes red in the face and runs out the room, you might think that what you're experiencing is not valid or severe enough to pay attention to. Isn't it funny how anxiety can make you feel like you're getting anxiety wrong?

That is why I want you to have an open mind and think back to the last time you had a social anxiety attack. Think about the way your body changed in response to its perceived danger. Think about the thoughts that went through your mind. What did you do to avoid the feeling or soothe it? Think about your unique social anxiety experience and go to your Workbook now. You'll be guided through the process of writing down the anatomy of YOUR experience so you can get to know and understand it better. Once you're done, come back and we'll continue.

Now that you have your unique social anxiety experience mapped out on paper take a look at it. How do you feel seeing it laid out in front of you? Putting words to an experience is a powerful tool. Not only does it help you easily recall the signs and symptoms you experience, but it removes some of the power that anxiety has over you. You've transformed a scary out-of-control experience into an understood, controlled one. You've just taken your power back.

Looking at what you've written down, how many of those symptoms matched the ones in this chapter? If it was more than a few of them, you might benefit from seeking a social anxiety disorder diagnosis. Don't let the thought of getting a label scare you. Remember, putting words to an experience is powerful.

SOCIAL ANXIETY VS. SOCIAL ANXIETY DISORDER

Getting a diagnosis for your social anxiety can help rule out any other potential problems. Many anxiety disorders will have different route causes and triggers. It's always nice to be sure of what you're dealing with.

You don't have to be defined by a diagnosis, but you can use it to your advantage by researching and learning as much as possible about the problem. When you have a name for it, you'll know what to look up.

If you have a severe or persistent case of social anxiety, it's important to receive a diagnosis to understand your experience better and qualify for professional help. Many people struggling with a severe case of social anxiety can potentially benefit from medications or a referral to a psychotherapist.

However, it's important to know that medication does not cure social anxiety. It only helps ease the symptoms until you've managed to work on the core of the problem or improve your coping skills. It is generally only recommended to people with such a severe case that the anxiety is significantly reducing their quality of life.

Maybe you've already received a diagnosis of social anxiety. That could be why you're reading this book. But just imagine if you didn't have a name for it, how would we have found each other? A diagnosis is not always a life sentence, especially not for social anxiety disorder. Social anxiety disorder can be resolved. You're not stuck with it, so embrace the diagnosis and use it for what it was intended for – receiving the right support.

If you don't have a diagnosis yet and you're thinking about getting an analysis, I want you to know that it sounds a lot scarier than it is. In truth, many psychiatric disorders are simply diagnosed by talking to a registered psychiatrist who will ask you questions and do an evaluation based on your answers.

While it can be daunting, try to feel comforted by their expertise in being able to help you. I also want you to know that if you don't qualify for a social anxiety disorder diagnosis, it doesn't mean that you don't experience social anxiety. It just means that you didn't meet all the requirements to benefit from a diagnosis. The diagnosis is generally there for people with a severe or persistent case of social anxiety.

For example, one of the main criteria to qualify for a diagnosis[3] includes having had symptoms of social anxiety for a minimum period of six months. So, anyone having social anxiety symptoms for under six months is still experiencing social anxiety, it just isn't persistent enough to meet the documented description of the condition.

Either way, anyone with social anxiety symptoms can benefit from the tools and methods throughout these books. So, don't worry if you aren't diagnosed, your experience is still valid and deserves to be taken seriously.

THE DAILY IMPACT OF SOCIAL ANXIETY

The impact social anxiety can have on your life is monumental. Even mild social anxiety can spoil special moments, cause negative thinking, and hold you back from making social connections. It can lead to unhappiness, unfulfillment, and most of all, loneliness.

Any form of social anxiety can rob you of the most valuable thing in this life: Love. I don't just mean romantic love, I mean the love between friends sharing exciting stories around the fire. The love you find in the smile of a stranger. The love of your dad wanting to take you to a live football game. The love that is found in the people wanting to connect with you every day. It's there, and without it, life can be pretty dull.

Social anxiety can have serious consequences on every aspect of your life. It can create problems wherever there are people involved, which is almost everywhere! Your job, your relationship, your family life, your friendships, every one of them can suffer under the pressure of social anxiety. Just think about it, you could:

- Struggle to focus at work because you work in an open office space.
- Miss out on dancing at a wedding because you didn't want to make a fool of yourself.
- Give up your ticket to a concert because the thought of the crowd scared you.
- Let your family down because you couldn't book a restaurant over the phone.
- Make a bad first impression because eye contact felt overwhelming.
- Avoid a new friendship even though you're lonely.

There are so many special moments, best friendships, and exciting experiences that social anxiety gets in the way of. But things can be different. No matter how severe your social anxiety is, even if you're on medication for it, there are so many things you can do, starting right now, to take your power back and live the life you dream of.

I want you to throw off your shoes and join the party conga line. I want you to hold your chin up and smile back when your eyes meet a stranger's. I want you to throw your arms up to "do the wave" with everyone at a concert. I want you to see a crowd of people, say "I'm safe," to yourself, and meet the friends you've been waiting for. I want you to experience the fulfillment of one of the most vital things for human happiness – <u>social connection.</u>

Things can be different. I know that they will be by the end of these books. Remember, you have to resolve the core of the problem to see a long-term improvement. And that's where these books will be your guide. So, if you're ready to meet your social self and never let social anxiety rob you of the love, connection, and fun you deserve, turn to chapter three now and let's get to work on transforming your very first enemy into an ally – your thoughts.

3

TRANSFORM YOUR THOUGHTS INTO ALLIES, NOT ENEMIES

Empowering Yourself For Social Interactions

I understand that the last chapter may have been difficult for you. It's never easy to look your fears in the face and embrace them. It's terrifying. I'm incredibly proud of you for making it through that. Now, you're here in chapter three, ready to give it your all, and I can't wait to show you the way.

You've already proven to yourself that you can identify and dissect your anxiety. Now, all you have to do is take action to resolve it. You're here because social anxiety is taking its toll on you and your social life. But social anxiety only has power in one place: Your mind.

Although social anxiety creates myriad emotions and sensations within the body, it originates from your thoughts. Your thoughts are the subconscious trigger for the experience. How do I know that? Because thoughts are linked to beliefs, and harmful beliefs are what cause social anxiety.

Let me repeat that: Harmful beliefs are what **causes** social anxiety.

Even though I'm a naturally shy and introverted person, I didn't always have social anxiety. Sure, I would go mute and sheepishly hide my face as my mom introduced me to new adults growing up, but the minute I was out on the playground, I was helpful, kind, and all I wanted was friends. I loved to laugh and play pretend with the other kids, and I had no problem standing up for people. My heart didn't race when I met someone new and my mind didn't spiral with all the potential mistakes I could make. I was just a normal, shy little girl.

As I got older and the safety of having my mom fell away, the security I had within myself slowly faded. The abandonment left me questioning myself and my worth. As the years went by, that questioning became a certainty. I wasn't important. At least that's what I thought at the time.

My demeanor changed. My shoulders began to slouch, my eyes looked at the ground instead of the sky, and my confidence was gone. In what seemed like an overnight shift, I became a natural target for bullies. Suddenly, social situations among my peers didn't feel so safe anymore. I now had an abundance of negative social interactions to choose from in my head when I thought about socializing. It wasn't long before I was on eggshells every time I spoke to someone.

I want you to see how a single traumatic event in my childhood could slowly create a reaction in my life, and eventually cause social anxiety. I was already a shy and sensitive child, but losing my confidence and self-worth had a snowball effect on the way I interacted with others. I suddenly didn't cope with conflict very well. I became the person being bullied, instead of the child standing up to them. And I no longer felt safe with any teacher who would raise their voice in class. The amount of "safe" people and social settings I had became smaller and smaller as the years went on.

You see, after I lost my mother, I built up false beliefs within myself. I believed that I wasn't lovable enough. I stopped being able to trust people and maintain any intimate connections, including friendships. Every time I made a friend, I believed that it wouldn't last, even though I deeply wished that it would. I secretly waited for them to betray my trust and when the friendship inevitably ended, as childhood friendships often do, the loss reinforced my belief that I didn't deserve to be loved.

Along with depression, anxiety, and other mental health issues, social anxiety became yet another rock in the baggage I carried throughout my life. My belief was that everyone who came into my life would eventually leave. Anytime something would happen, like the loss of a pet, or a friend moving towns, it reinforced my belief.

This belief triggered thoughts that damaged my ability to socialize.

"The whole friendship was a lie."

"They never truly loved me."

"I'm not good enough."

The belief triggered negative thought patterns that targeted my self-esteem and continued to break me down. My mind became my worst enemy and like links to the same chain, every problem I faced fed off of each other, holding the shackles of my unhappiness in place.

Only when I could unravel the web of mental illness I was stuck in could I trace back the source of my problems. Among other things, losing my mom was a major catalyst, and the false beliefs that came next kept me trapped for years. Each negative social interaction reinforced my negative thinking patterns, and the avoidance cycle was set in motion. But once I figured out where my mind was going wrong, I could backtrack and make sense of it all.

You see, your social anxiety doesn't happen out of the blue. Even though it can feel very confusing and come on unexpectedly, there is always a root cause. Finding the root cause and identifying where your thoughts are going wrong is vital to seeing progress.

You have to start at the source for all the other methods in these books to fall into place.

Social anxiety originates in the mind, it is built on false beliefs. These beliefs manipulate your thoughts and control your reaction to social situations. The beauty in that is if the problem is in your mind, the solution is in your mind as well. That's what this chapter is all about. You're going to learn how to fight negative thoughts with productive ones. You'll learn how to make your thoughts go from enemies to allies. Your thoughts are YOUR thoughts. You have the power to take back control and become conscious of your thinking patterns.

IDENTIFYING NEGATIVE THOUGHTS

I don't want you to worry about which false beliefs are driving your thoughts just yet. Once you learn to identify which of your thoughts are helpful and which are harmful, you'll start to notice a pattern. Over time the false beliefs and the experiences that caused them will surface. When you look back on what your internal narrative has been saying all this time, it will become clear what beliefs have been holding you back. So, for now, just focus on your thoughts.

It's easy to distinguish a negative thought from a positive one. The trick is to become receptive to how your thoughts make you *feel*. A negative thought will bring you down, spiral into more negative thinking, and make you doubt yourself. A positive thought will lift you up, open your mind to possibilities, and bring you a sense of clarity. If you feel like running away from the thought, it is very likely that the thought is negative. Let's clarify it further:

Negative Thoughts

Thoughts that are false and do not serve you well. These include thoughts that are negative about you, others, and the world. To identify them, consider whether or not they:

- Trigger negative emotions.
- Trigger more negative thinking.
- Trigger a fight or flight response.
- Feed into false beliefs.
- Cause you to question yourself.

Positive Thoughts

Thoughts that are true and improve your outlook on life. These are not thoughts that invalidate your struggles but rather ones that genuinely uplift you. To identify them, consider whether or not they:

- Trigger positive emotions.
- Keep your thoughts stable and linear.
- Bring you a sense of peace, relief, or satisfaction.
- Build up a beneficial and true narrative within you.
- Give you clarity.

Before I continue, I want you to know that thoughts are not inherently "good" or "bad." Thoughts can only affect us the way that we allow them to. If you give your thoughts too much validity and you entertain them no matter what they are, you give your thoughts more power than they deserve.

Your thoughts are there to serve you. They are not coming from some well of unknown truths hidden within yourself. Thoughts come from your stream of consciousness and it's your hard-wired thinking patterns that decide what kind of thoughts you're having. You must know that just because you have a thought doesn't mean it's true. Our minds can use false beliefs based on painful experiences to twist our thoughts and use them to feed a negative narrative within us. You can't always trust your own thinking.

You also do not have to entertain negative thoughts. Once you can identify which thoughts are serving you and which thoughts are feeding a negative narrative within you, you can begin to shift and reframe them. If you're still unsure what negative thoughts can sound like, here are some examples:

- I can never do anything right.
- No one loves me.
- I deserve the pain that I feel.
- It's impossible for me to make friends.
- Life's unfair, and I just need to toughen up.
- I'm too sensitive.
- I'm such an idiot. I always make stupid mistakes.
- There's nothing wrong with me. Everyone else is the problem.

- I'm better off alone in this world.

None of these thoughts inspire action to solve a problem. Each one perpetuates a negative narrative within the person thinking them. Negative thoughts like these form part of a lack or limiting mindset where you stop being able to see potential and possibilities in life. Thinking in this way blocks you from evolving and learning from negative experiences. These thoughts allow you to be a victim of your circumstances and fortify a belief that you are powerless.

On the other hand, positive thoughts can sound like this:

- I can handle life's difficulties.
- I am worthy of love and friendships.
- I haven't had much luck with friendships. Maybe I just haven't met the right people yet.
- Life can be cruel, but there is so much beauty in it too.
- I'm responsible for the role that I play in my problems.
- I'm really struggling right now. What can I do to improve my circumstances?
- Great things take time, I need to be patient right now.
- I'm a sensitive person, so let me be more cautious about how I speak to myself.

Can you see how these thoughts are not shaming negative feelings but rather helping to support a solution to the problem? Instead of breaking you down and putting a block between you and progress, these types of thoughts can help to encourage you and fortify positive beliefs about your abilities and yourself. These types of thoughts form part of a growth mindset, where you think in a way that allows for growth, possibilities, and constant self-improvement. They allow you to feel empowered and capable in your life. You need to speak to yourself kindly in this way and exercise patience with yourself if you're struggling.

In a social setting, your thoughts will either make or break you. You can have anxiety and feel uncomfortable while out amongst people, but if your thoughts are breaking you down and creating more conflict within you, your negative thinking will cause you to retreat into yourself and become overwhelmed. But if your thoughts are building you up and encouraging you, you will start to feel supported by your own mind and build up your self-esteem.

I'm going to dive into the importance of confidence in chapter 4, but for now, I need you to understand that your thoughts will be the number one element transforming you into the social butterfly you know you are beneath your anxiety. Confidence is your key to healing social anxiety, but you can't build it without fixing your thinking first.

COGNITIVE DISTORTIONS: HOW YOUR THOUGHTS CAN SPOIL A GOOD THING

Some common problems that happen with your thinking when you experience social anxiety are an array of cognitive distortions. These are ways that your thoughts spiral your anxiety until it is out of control. You have to be aware that your anxiety is ruled by a misbelief about social interactions. Cognitive distortions are your anxiety's way of sticking around and reinforcing this false belief you've acquired. They include:

- **Black and white thinking:** A thinking pattern that makes you think in absolutes. You either see things one way or another and have no room for gray areas. For example, if you think that you are a good person, then once you make a mistake, you suddenly think you are a bad person. You leave no room for being a good person who has made a mistake.

- **Catastrophizing:** A cognitive distortion that causes you to ruminate about the worst outcome of a situation. It is a thinking pattern that often starts with one negative thought and snowballs into the ultimate worst-case scenario. For example, if you are late for work and you accidentally spill coffee on your shirt then suddenly start thinking about all the repercussions in an irrational way. You start by thinking about the time it's going to waste to change your shirt, then you imagine your boss yelling at you for being late, then you imagine him calling you into his office and firing you. Then, you imagine being jobless and losing your house. In an instant, the thoughts go from spilling coffee on your shirt to you being homeless without a job.

- **Overgeneralization:** This is a common thinking pattern that can feed into false beliefs by making generalized assumptions and drawing conclusions that do not take the whole story into account. For example, you get invited to a wedding and you suddenly start stressing about having to face all the people and family that will be there. Your mind starts coming up with generalized conclusions to back up a false belief you have. Maybe you haven't seen some of the family for a long time and you start thinking things like, "That side of the family has never liked me." or "They only invited me because I'm related to the groom. They wouldn't care if I didn't come." These conclusions are not based on any real evidence or fact, they are broad conclusions that only solidify a negative belief about family.

Cognitive distortions are simply patterns that your mind has become trapped in. They are triggered by a false belief you have hidden within yourself and it is these thoughts that trigger the anxiety to surface and become out of control.

You might even experience all three cognitive distortions in one unpleasant situation where your social anxiety is triggered. Perhaps you are going to host a family dinner and you've known about it for weeks. As the event draws near, your anxiety slowly rises. Then, a week before the event, your mind is already playing tricks on you. You catastrophize about how you might forget the roast in the oven and ruin the whole dinner by not having any food to serve everyone. You might hear your thoughts say things like, "Mom is only coming over to lecture me about my failures in life. She's always judging me." Maybe you even stop being able to rationalize the gray areas of how your family is and you think, "Family dinners are the worst. They always end in disaster."

In this scenario, your anxiety has gotten the better of you. It's made you believe that there is no chance that the dinner might be a nice experience. It's made you assume things about family members, and it's left no possibilities open in your mind for having a successful dinner. You've created a block for yourself against having a good time. Now, anything that goes wrong regarding the event will reinforce your belief that family dinners are a nightmare. You will likely be anxious the entire time leading up to the event as you anticipate disaster and confrontation.

Now I want you to imagine that the anxiety didn't have power over you. Imagine what would happen if you challenged every negative thought and replaced it with something helpful instead. Imagine saying, "Yes, family dinners can be chaotic, but it's nothing I can't handle." Imagine being open to having a wholesome experience with your family instead of blocking off the potential for a good time. There might still be stressful moments during the event, but your mind will start to see and remember the positives instead of only seeing the things that go wrong. Can you see how it's possible to transform life by shifting the way you think?

In order to break the cycle of negative thinking, you have to realize that these thinking traps are not real. Your mind has been trained through painful experiences to think in these ways and your anxiety perpetuates them. They don't hold any weight unless you allow them to. You can stop them in their tracks by becoming aware of them and using conscious thinking to take your power back.

AUTOMATIC THOUGHTS VS. CONSCIOUS THINKING

For most of my life, I was a victim of my thoughts. I would attack myself in my mind and tear my self-esteem to shreds. Although I would try and fight back I couldn't help but believe the things my mind would come up with. Very soon, my lack of confidence was reflected in every interaction I had with others. My thoughts were out of control, and as a result, my anxiety was out of control.

Only once I grew an awareness for my thoughts, and gained control over them through conscious thinking and redirection, did I start to fix the narrative I had for myself and begin to thrive in every social interaction I had.

To shift your thinking, you need to become aware of it. There is a difference between thinking on autopilot and actively being in control of your thoughts. When your thoughts are on autopilot, they are automatic. But when you are actively engaging with your thoughts with the intention to listen, identify, and shift them, your thoughts are becoming conscious.

When I talk about conscious thinking, I don't mean thinking while you're awake. What I mean by <u>conscious thinking is your ability to be self-aware and consciously form new and improved thoughts to nurture better thinking patterns</u>. Conscious thinking is how you will act on your negative thoughts once you identify them.

I need you to know that this is going to be a process. It's not going to happen by the end of this chapter. Fixing your thought patterns is going to take time and consistent practice. Once you are aware of your thoughts, they aren't going to affect you as severely as they once did, but it won't stop the thoughts from coming. Your automatic thinking will continue, but it won't have the same impact as it did before. When you learn to sift through your automatic thoughts, you become the conscious driver behind what those thoughts mean to you and how you will sort them.

Becoming the conscious driver of your automatic thoughts includes a few things. It includes becoming aware of your thoughts and thinking patterns, questioning the validity of your thoughts, sorting your thoughts into different categories such as positive,

Conscious thinking is your ability to be self-aware and consciously form new and improved thoughts to nurture better thinking patterns

negative, and neutral, and reframing your thoughts to nurture positive thinking patterns.

I want you to take a moment right now to practice becoming a conscious thinker. Start by closing your eyes and taking a deep breath. Allow your automatic thoughts to continue and do nothing for a moment besides observing them. I want you to imagine your thoughts like clouds passing through a blue sky. Try not to attach any meaning to the thoughts, just observe them.

You might see thoughts like, "This is stupid," "What's the point of all this?" or, "Am I doing this right?" Don't try to fight them, just observe them. By observing your thoughts in this way, you are becoming the conscious observer of your thoughts. You're viewing your thoughts as they deserve to be viewed, as clouds passing through – they aren't always going to have meaning. I want you to get comfortable seeing your thoughts like clouds so that when you have a negative thought your instinct is to observe it without judgment instead of allowing it to consume you in darkness.

Again, your thoughts aren't always going to have meaning, so just observe them and let them pass.

The next step to becoming a conscious thinker is to start sorting your thoughts as they come. You already know how to identify a negative thought, and you're going to get much better at it with practice and time. Next time you start to notice your thoughts becoming negative, I want you to try and observe them like you did just now. See the thoughts for what they are: thoughts. They are nothing more than that. They can't hurt you if you don't allow them to, and you need to become comfortable questioning their validity.

As a conscious thinker, you don't see thoughts as fact anymore, you observe them, question their validity if they seem harmful, and you sort them. Once you have identified a negative thought, like a storm cloud passing through a blue sky, question it. Ask yourself, "Is this true?" If you aren't sure whether it's true or not, try to think about what the purpose of that thought is. If there is no direct purpose for the thought other than to bring you down or catastrophize a situation, or if it's overly general, it probably isn't true. Take that thought, and categorize it for yourself as junk.

I want you to start seeing your negative thoughts as garbage and remind yourself where they belong whenever you have them. They are rubbish thoughts and they deserve to be discarded like putting an old document into the trash folder of a computer. Don't waste your time on it, just throw it aside.

Instead of giving your thoughts power by entertaining everything they say, call them out for what they are and remind yourself where they belong whenever they resurface. Seeing as your negative thoughts are often caused by false beliefs, chances are you are going to start noticing negative thoughts that resurface and repeat themselves.

Over time, as you become familiar with which thought patterns reemerge in your mind, and you continue to remind yourself that those thoughts are rubbish, they will start to lose strength and validity within you. You have then successfully started breaking down an old, hardwired thought pattern. But to make your conscious thinking abilities more powerful and long-lasting, I'm going to teach you how to reframe your negative thoughts to shift them forever.

Your Thoughts Are Your Guide

As a useful interjection, I want to come back to the beliefs that are causing negative thinking for you. Now that you are starting to identify your negative thinking patterns, you might start to notice beliefs attached to them.

For example, if you notice thoughts like "I'm such an idiot." "I can never do anything right." or "There I go, messing things up as usual." you might be struggling with a false belief that you are not capable. Or, if you notice thoughts like, "No one cares about me." "I'm better off alone." or "I'm not good enough for friends to stick around." you might be dealing with a false belief regarding your worth.

I want you to take a moment right now and open up your Workbook. Write down the negative thoughts that you have noticed within yourself and try to see if there is a consistent theme between them. If you can identify a theme or pattern, write down what you think it might be then come back to me. You can continue adding to this page over time to keep track and uncover more false beliefs that you might be struggling with. False beliefs can be anything that looks like this:

- I'm worthless.
- I'm not capable enough.
- I'm not lovable.
- I don't belong anywhere.
- I'm a failure.

Once you have identified a false belief, it may be clear already where that belief came from. But if it isn't, I want you to keep in mind that somewhere over the course of your life, something happened that sparked this false belief within you. You don't have to try and get to the bottom of it right away. Allow it to slowly reveal itself along your healing journey. Facing your core reason for a false belief is often very painful and difficult. I want you to be aware that there is a cause, and that at some point, when you are ready, it may resurface and you can then work to resolve it. You do not, by any means, need to push yourself to heal that core reason just yet. Be patient with yourself, and know that this recovery process will take time.

If you are ready to become a conscious thinker that is unaffected by negative thinking, keep reading. It's time to develop your conscious thinking action plan and take steps towards healing your negative thought patterns forever.

YOUR CONSCIOUS THINKING ACTION PLAN

The good news about negative thinking patterns is that they aren't set in stone. You have the power to transform your thoughts from enemies to allies. Instead of breaking you down and keeping you small, you can use your thoughts to build your confidence and encourage growth.

I'm going to teach you how to use your thoughts as a powerful tool in overcoming negative thought patterns. With time, effort, a little trust in yourself, and these methods, it won't be long before you feel your false beliefs start to shift as well. The goal is not to simply detach from your thoughts and carry on in a state of numbness, but to rather shift your perspective about yourself and social settings to a place where your confidence shines through any anxiety you may still feel. I'm here to teach you methods that are going to help you for the long term. If you are ready to try them and stick to them, let's create your conscious thinking action plan.

Depending on what false beliefs you are dealing with, your action plan might look different to someone else's. Regardless, try to see how you can make use of each of the following steps.

Step 1: Challenge Negative Thoughts

When you are faced with an anxiety-inducing situation, and you feel your thoughts getting out of control, start by stepping into the role of a conscious observer. Remember the exercise that you did previously in this chapter and start observing your thoughts like clouds passing through the blue sky of your mind.

Observe the thoughts that you are having and start to question, or challenge them. Challenging negative thoughts takes away their power because you are no longer entertaining them. You are acknowledging that they are simply thoughts, and you decide whether or not they are meaningful to you. Challenge their validity, and make a decision about where they belong. Are they trash, or do they hold some truth?

Step 2: Reframe Negative Thoughts

If a negative thought holds some weight for you and you are struggling to get rid of it, this is where conscious redirection, or reframing, comes in. Take the thought in your mind and figure out a way that you can transform it into something that is more true and beneficial.

For example, if you have the thought, "No one ever listens to me. I'm invisible." try to see how you can rephrase the thought for yourself to make it more true. Try something like, "I struggle to speak up for myself, and as a result I feel invisible. What can I do to help people hear me better?" If you can change the thoughts you're having into thoughts that are not absolute and encourage a solution, you're going to keep hold of your power rather than allowing anxiety to take over. Instead of:

- "No one loves me" try, "I'm struggling to feel loved and accepted by people."

- "I'm a failure" try "I can only do my best and that's enough."

- "Why do I always make a fool of myself?" try "My awkwardness doesn't need to define me or hold me back."

- "All my friends hate me" try "These friends are often upset with me, either I'm doing something hurtful to them or I need to find better friends."

It may take some getting used to, but practice reframing your thoughts to reflect reality rather than your anxious beliefs. Of course, you can't always stop a thought in its tracks or know that you're about to think something harmful. The trick to reframing negative thoughts is to follow them up with a more helpful, genuine thought. Over time, positive thinking will become a habit and you will automatically start to think better.

Remember, negative thinking is a thinking pattern that was created by negative experiences which formed false beliefs. Your thinking patterns were created by your experiences, they are not an unchangeable variable in who you are. You can change them for the better, and you can change them for good.

Step 3: Practice Positive Self-Talk

Much like reframing negative thoughts, you need to practice speaking to yourself more positively in general. The way you treat yourself and speak to yourself is often directly related to how you feel at any given time. Your relationship with yourself is governed by the things you say to yourself and the way you show up for yourself during difficult times.

I want you to give this some thought right now. What kind of tone do you use when you speak to yourself? What kind of words do you use? Do you call yourself names when you mess something up? If you're struggling with anxiety on any level, I can guess that your inner voice isn't always the most forgiving.

To minimize your anxiety and become more confident in yourself, you have to, and I mean *have* to, start speaking to yourself like you would a friend. Remember, YOU are your biggest support system in life. No one is going to show up for you better than you can show up for yourself. So, the next time you hear yourself saying something like, "God, I'm such an idiot!" or "Well done." in a sarcastic tone, stop for a moment and ask yourself, "Would I say this to a friend?" And if that isn't enough, consider how you'd feel if someone else spoke to you like that.

If you'd be angry with someone else for saying something to you, don't you dare go and speak to yourself like that. You deserve better, and you'd be surprised how much more supported and happy you'll feel if your inner voice, the one that you can't escape, becomes your biggest ally. Just how you have to shift your thinking, you have to shift the tone and words of your inner voice. Start treating yourself with kindness and respect.

Step 4: Slowly Shift False Beliefs

Negative thinking patterns and negative self talk both originate from harmful beliefs. If you don't believe you're worthy of respect and kindness, why would your inner voice and your thoughts say nice things to you?

The good news is, all you have to do to shift false beliefs within yourself is fix the symptoms of false beliefs. If your false beliefs are manifesting in cognitive distortions (the nasty thinking traps of catastrophizing, blank-and-white thinking, and overgeneralization), negative self-talk, and general negative thinking patterns, becoming a conscious thinker will automatically start to unravel harmful beliefs.

For example, if you don't believe you are worthy of love and respect, but you start challenging negative thoughts that solidify that belief, you are in turn challenging the belief itself. The same goes for positive thinking. If you start practicing positive thinking, and you talk to yourself with love and respect, you are proving to yourself that you *are* worthy. You don't need to do anything to the belief directly, by challenging and changing the thoughts and behaviors caused by the belief, it will slowly start to fade away as you reinforce newer, healthier ones. You have to prove the belief wrong for it to change.

Step 5: Try Cognitive Behavioral Therapy

If you are struggling to restructure your thinking patterns on your own, cognitive behavioral therapy (CBT) is a great way to introduce and reinforce the practice of "fixing" negative thinking with the help of an experienced therapist.

The principles of CBT are much the same as the ones discussed throughout this chapter. They include the principles that:

- Our core beliefs about ourselves, the world, and the future affect our psychological health.

- We, as humans, have a tendency to focus on the negative more easily, creating irrational cognitive distortions that warp our view of reality.

- Our minds are capable of automatic negative thoughts that can affect our moods and behaviors, but these thoughts are only a habit not a fixed condition.

The main belief within CBT is that thoughts affect our emotions and therefore our behaviors. With the help of a cognitive behavioral therapist, or psychologist, it teaches how to positively influence your thoughts in order to improve your emotions and behaviors.

In regards to social anxiety, participating in CBT can help you talk through some of the negative social experiences you go through and work to resolve the thoughts which make these experiences overwhelming for you. It can help you see your thoughts and behaviors in a new light so that your emotions are more positive and manageable in a social setting.

You see, there are so many tools at your disposal. You can let out a sigh of relief knowing that there is so much you can do to overcome your anxiety and find joy amongst the people that you love. You don't have to be damned to a lifetime of social awkwardness, you can consciously decide right now that you are going to see a change. Don't worry, you won't have to do it alone. We are nowhere near done! Mastering your thoughts is the first step, but there is so much more.

Remember what I said about confidence? It's going to be the key to healing your social anxiety. Now that your negative thinking is on a leash, it's time to turn to chapter four and learn how to never worry about embarrassing yourself, being too quiet, or not knowing what to say again.

Before you do, spend a moment to ensure that your exercises in the Workbook are complete. There are several powerful questions contained in there that provide thoughtful structure around the management of your thoughts.

TURN SELF-DOUBT INTO SELF-CONFIDENCE

Practices To Recognize Your Strengths
& Celebrate Your Imperfections

Sitting on the bleachers set up on the school stage, I watched in awe as Priscilla stood under the spotlight. She was talented and beautiful, her voice was butter to the ears. We were performing "Part Of That World" from The Little Mermaid, and never before had I resonated more with that song. Priscilla was Ariel, and I was an urchin in the background.

In comparison, Priscilla and I were both strong singers, but she had something I could only dream of – confidence. She pranced about the stage in the flashy mermaid costume her mother had hand-sewn for her, while I tried my best to blend into the "coral reef" wearing a cheerleader's pom-pom on my head. As I heard her belt out the final verse of the song, I embodied every emotion the lyrics conveyed. "Wish I could be, part of that world" rang on repeat in my head on the car ride home as I imagined myself as Ariel, confidently captivating the stage.

After three solid years of weekly ballet lessons, you'd think I would have had plenty of opportunity to take the lead in the many live performances I danced and sang as a child. But although I always dreamed of it, the dream didn't translate to reality. I lacked confidence and my self-esteem only weakened with age. Lead roles are usually given to kids who have undoubting stage presence. But without confidence, you might as well be a shadow.

Self-confidence is the thing that makes you stand out in a crowd of people. It's that glorious essence you feel from someone who really knows and loves themselves. They seem to glow with it. I'm sure growing up, you can name the kids who always seemed to just get it right. The kids who naturally claimed captain of the football team, debate team champion, or lead role.

I want you to know the secret behind their success. Sure, they may have been talented and hardworking, but they had something the other kids didn't. The secret sauce that made these kids shine was their brilliant belief in themselves. They didn't, for one second, doubt whether they were good enough. They *knew* it.

I'm not trying to generalize here. I'm sure there are plenty of stories of triumph where the shy kid made captain or the girl on the bleachers made the lead. But it's only natural for people to see greatness in those who are confident enough to share it with the world. I'm also not saying that you need to be some cocky, outgoing person to get what you want out of life.

What I am saying is that you need to awaken to the value that you are holding back from the world. You CAN be the shy girl, the quiet guy, or the introvert and still capture the attention you want when you walk into a room. You don't have to change who you are, you simply have to learn how to make your unique and wonderful presence brighter with confidence.

Only after I started putting in the work to see my self-worth again and build my confidence up from the ground did I do what I always wanted to. I performed live for the first time as part of a duo, front and center, and saw the faces of the audience light up as we began to harmonize the chorus. I was nervous but my self-confidence was already at a level where I didn't care if I messed up. I knew that if I enjoyed myself and gave it my best effort, that energy would translate through my song. Let this prove that you don't have to be "born with it" to have a strong presence. I am that "shy girl" that went on to get the lead, eventually.

That glow. That essence of captivating energy that makes you just want to be around someone isn't always a born trait. Self-confidence is something that you can grow. You might even be surprised to learn that many of the kids who seemed to have it all growing up had help growing their self-confidence too. Maybe they had a parent who pushed them out of their comfort zone and encouraged them to go after what they wanted. Maybe they grew up being reminded how much they were worth. And maybe they had parents whose incredible self-confidence rubbed off on them. Maybe *you* were one of those kids but lost your confidence somehow.

There are so many factors as to why some people have better self-confidence and others don't. But the most important thing you need to absorb from this is that confidence can be learned.

No, you don't have to have had the world's greatest parents growing up to have self-confidence now. It doesn't matter how low your self-esteem is or what you've been through, you can recover the spark of confidence you have hidden within you. I know something tough might have happened to you that dimmed your flame and robbed you of your place in the spotlight. But it's never too late to heal. Social anxiety is just a confidence-deficit.

Let me repeat that: Social anxiety is a confidence-deficit.

Without self-confidence, your presence becomes small and you fade into the background of social settings. It's difficult to feel wanted and celebrated socially when you aren't sure whether people notice you at all. Even if you have what others see as a gleaming social life, the amount of energy and effort it takes to keep up the facade is draining you, it's a sign your inner fire of confidence needs rekindling.

I don't want you to spend another minute feeling small. I want this book to be your ignition. I want you to take whatever hope you have left for finding relief and put your trust in me for the duration of these pages. It's your turn to look in the mirror and see the glow for yourself. I need you to **feel** what it's like to captivate people and be celebrated wherever you go. But it has to start with YOU.

No one else is going to see your worth if you don't. You can't expect others to embrace and love you if you don't love yourself first. Take to this chapter with an open mind and entertain the thought that you have immense value. Your self-esteem and self-confidence are siblings in your journey to overcoming social anxiety. It's time for you to be brave and see your worth for what it is – a firework lighting up the night sky. You have an explosion of brilliance waiting to light up every room you enter. Let me show you how to unleash it.

SELF-ESTEEM VS. SELF-CONFIDENCE

There is a difference between self-esteem and self-confidence. You need both in order to heal your social anxiety.

Self-confidence is the trust that you have in yourself and what you're capable of. Even the word "confidence" means "to trust" in Latin. So, if you have the feeling that you can't trust yourself and your ability to handle whatever life throws at you, you're naturally going to feel anxious as you anticipate becoming swamped by the problems of life.

Similarly, your self-esteem is also a perception you have of yourself, except this time, it's your confidence in your own value. A lack of self-esteem means you lack self-worth or a positive perception of yourself.

You can also lack self-esteem and self-confidence at the same time. If you look closely at your level of social anxiety, I can guarantee it is almost the direct opposite of your level of confidence in YOU. The more anxiety you have, the less confidence you are likely to have as well. But it isn't the anxiety that has affected your confidence, it's your lack of confidence that has created the anxiety.

This is why some people who have a natural confidence about them can sometimes also suffer from social anxiety — their self-esteem has been wounded. It is also how someone with healthy self-esteem can still experience the beating heartbeat and sweaty palms — their self-confidence is lacking.

Wherever you feel that you are lacking, even if you're struggling without both, your social anxiety experience is valid. There is a reason why you don't feel comfortable in a social environment, but before you worry about your external environment, I need you to focus on your internal environment.

Along with fixing your thoughts, which have had an effect on the false beliefs you have about yourself and the world, fixing your confidence is the next vital step to healing social anxiety. After already working on your thinking patterns, you are ready to start working on your perception of yourself.

But it isn't the anxiety that has affected your confidence, it's your lack of confidence that has created the anxiety.

The good news is that each exercise and inner shift you successfully go through throughout this book makes the next step easier. Every method I teach here works with the next like a cog in the wheel of your well-being. I want you to see them as parts of the same whole. Each thing you do to heal is not separate. If you trust the process and give each concept and exercise your full attention, you will start to notice a cumulative effect. So, to build on the positive thinking patterns you've been working on since chapter three, I want you to start building your self-confidence and self-esteem.

You need to stop and recognize where your strengths lie and celebrate that. No more undermining what you are capable of. I need you to give yourself the benefit of the doubt and start putting your focus on the things you CAN do rather than those you can't.

There are many strategies you can use to recognize your own worth and capabilities. But the most important thing you can do is become open-minded to the fact that there are things you're good at and things you aren't. There's nothing wrong with that. The beauty of every person is the combination of the two. As social creatures, having strengths and weaknesses brings us together.

To recognize what your strengths are, you need to become receptive to them. Listen to what people say about you. Notice when you do a great job at something and compare it to the times when you fail. If you are receptive to your strengths, it won't be long before you pick up on patterns and discover what they are. Go to your Workbook now and let the exercise there give you a much-needed confidence boost.

PROGRESS OVER PERFECTION

This is such an important concept

To really embrace your strengths and give yourself the credit you deserve, I want to address your concern about perfection. You might think, "But I don't have a problem with perfectionism." And to that, I have to ask you: Do you worry about making a mistake in the public eye? Do you obsess over ensuring your outfit is "good enough" before going out with your friends? Are you concerned about making a fool of yourself in conversation? Do you beat yourself up for saying the wrong thing or stumbling over your words? If you answered "yes" to any of the above or can imagine doing something similar, perfection has a role to play.

Perfectionism is the source of self-criticism. It can take on many forms, but the one that I want to address today is the expectations you place on yourself and every social interaction you have. Letting perfectionism rule your social life is the bane to its success. You have to let go of your hidden need for things to be under control in order to embrace the imperfections of life fully.

If you can embrace life in all its imperfect glory, you won't be so quick to beat yourself up over any old mistake. You'll learn to laugh in the face of embarrassment instead of letting fear consume you. Life is not as serious as we often make it. If you can learn to let go a little and be realistic about the potential outcome of certain situations, you're going to loosen up a whole lot.

I need you to become comfortable with the fact that you might say the wrong thing or even trip and fall. If you can accept embarrassment before it happens, it won't matter what mishaps you encounter because you already know that it's not such a big deal to slip up. You need to check your expectations and make sure you're being realistic. Everyone makes mistakes, it's okay to look silly sometimes. Awkwardness is more common than you think, and it often doesn't have the implications we decide it has. I can assure you most people are too busy worrying about themselves to notice your imperfections. So, get comfortable being perfectly imperfect.

I know it isn't easy to get out of your own head and let go. But as you build your self-confidence, you will become more comfortable with failure. Failure only has power over you if you place your worth and perception of yourself on your ability to never fail. But that would be unrealistic. That is why you need to start seeing your worth as unshakable. But before you can do that, you need to love yourself and decide that you deserve to treat yourself better.

BUILDING SELF-CONFIDENCE WITH SELF-CARE

Think about self-confidence like a lemon seed. If you put a lemon seed in clay, it doesn't matter how much you water it, the seed will never germinate. And even if the seed does germinate, it will not grow into a fruitful lemon tree.

However, plant the lemon seed in nutrient-rich soil and it won't take much effort for the seed to sprout and transform into a glorious yellow explosion.

Sure, it will take time, but the richer the soil is, the less effort it will take for the tree to survive.

In the same way, you can't expect your self-confidence to grow and become lush if your inner environment is as suffocating as clay. You need to have a nurturing inner environment for the seed of self-confidence to breathe, grow, and thrive.

But what does a rich inner environment consist of? It consists of a genuine self-love that you have put effort into experiencing. Without self-love, your inner world is barren and dark. However, with self-love, your inner world is beautiful, bright, and full of life. You need to nurture a healthy inner world of self-love if you want to grow your confidence.

Once you have a rich inner world full of self-love and kindness, you won't have to try hard to have self-confidence. Everything you do to grow your confidence will be like water to a seed. And because your inner environment is healthy and thriving, your efforts will not go to waste. Your confidence will outgrow your wildest expectations because you love yourself enough to know that you are capable and you are worth it.

Self-care is the greatest tool to nurture a healthy inner environment. Even the act of self-care itself is proof that you love and value yourself to some degree. I need you to prioritize your self-care practice if you want to see progress. It is an invaluable asset to recovering from social anxiety. There is also no one-size-fits-all rule as to what good self-care looks like. The only guideline you need to consider is whether or not your self-care is genuinely nurturing or whether it's secretly harmful.

Self-care is an incredible tool to calm you down and help you feel safe. I want you to consider self-care as your emergency aid to a social anxiety attack. Use it to bring yourself down to a more functional level before you take action on thoughts that do not serve you. Love yourself enough to break the pattern of self-sabotage and replace the way you cope right now with self-care exercises instead. If you aren't sure what good self-care looks like, try some of the exercises below. You'll find them repeated in your Workbook with added prompts and room for your journaling too.

Self-Care Exercises For Social Anxiety

- **Healthy distractions:** This can look like watching a funny movie, baking your favorite treat, spending time with an animal, or doing anything you love that is highly engaging and can take your mind off of spiraling thoughts.

- **Journaling:** There are many ways to use a journal. You can do a stream-of-consciousness journal where you write down everything you think as it comes. You can try following some journal prompts to help provoke introspection or problem-solving. Or you can simply open up your journal and write down the experience that is bugging you. Open up your Workbook now, and see the journal prompts waiting for you. You can use these whenever you feel like you need an outlet. Try one right now if you must!

- **Rest and repair:** Any activity that contributes to your rest or recovery after a stressful bout of social anxiety. This can include pouring a bath, lighting some candles and snuggling up with a book, eating a wholesome meal, or anything else that nourishes your body, mind, and soul.

- **Movement:** Sometimes, moving your body is the only way to fully release the emotions you've built up during a socially anxious moment. You can go for a walk, put on your favorite music and dance alone in your room, wiggle your body and imagine releasing the energy, or do any form of exercise that feels good to you.

- **Reaching out for help:** Just because you struggle with social anxiety doesn't mean you can't reach out to people you love for support. You can reach out in whatever way is comfortable for you. This can include asking your partner for a hug, sending your best friend a text message, calling your most trusted parent or guardian, or emailing your therapist.

Engage in self-care activities to help you calm down and return to baseline quickly. They are here to help soothe your fight-or-flight response, and they will help build a sense of self-love within you. You can also do them whenever you feel generally overwhelmed or drained by life. They are here to bring you peace and help you reconnect with yourself in the most loving way. Self-care is the ultimate tool for supporting yourself through difficult times.

THE SECRET OF SUPPORT

You might have heard how important a good support system is in life. I'm not going to deny that. A good support system is priceless and can help you feel more capable and confident in the face of struggle. With a good support system, you know that there will always be people who can back you up, listen to you, and support you in finding a solution to a problem.

You decide who you consider a part of your support system based on who you can trust and rely on the most. It can be anyone in your life that you are close to. Your support system is the people who you would go to in a crisis.

It can include:

- Family
- Friends
- Partners
- Work colleagues
- Professional support
- And even pets

I want you to go to your Workbook now and write down the first 5 names that come to your mind when you think about picking up the phone and calling someone for emotional support or help. Who are the people in your life that you can fully rely on to be there for you, listen to your side of the story, and offer comfort and support willingly? Write their names down and their contact information. *Please do this. It's really helpful*

Your support system is important to your healing journey, but it can only serve you if you reach out and contact the people who are a part of it in times of need. However, a good support system can help you feel supported without needing to call someone at all. Knowing they're there can give you an amazing sense of confidence for tackling hardships.

If your support system is small, you can consider expanding it over time by seeking professional help. Mental health experts are there to support you and are some of the most equipped people to do so. You can start seeing a therapist or counselor and add them to the list of people you can count on. Besides, once your social anxiety is under control, your support system will likely grow as your friendships bloom.

Your support system can also include people online, like the friends you make in the LearnWell Community.

Now I want to let you in on a secret to taking your support system to the next level. In fact, everyone in your support system right now could disappear and you'd still cope.

The secret to an unbreakable support system is YOU.

No one can support you better than yourself. Without your own support, you rely on others to pick you up when you're down. Don't get me wrong, we all need help. But if you are not an integral part of your own support system, you give up your power and leave your fate in the hands of others. However, if you support yourself, it won't matter if everyone you know and love suddenly disappears; you'll still be okay – at least for some time.

I'm not trying to scare you with the thought of having no one. What I'm trying to show you is the importance of your own love and support in life. Many people don't have a good support system and that can make life very difficult and very lonely. But, if you don't step up for yourself first, attracting and building a great support system will be even more difficult. If you can show up for yourself in times of need and trust yourself to handle difficult situations, it won't matter if you're completely alone; you'll always make it through tough times.

I'm also not saying that doing things alone is the easier way to go. Nor am I saying that you don't need people in your life to be happy. There is a well of benefits to having a strong support system. Some benefits include:

- Decreased stress and anxiety.
- A sense of belonging.
- Improved coping skills.
- A higher sense of wellness.
- Strong emotional support.
- Better self-esteem.
- And even increased longevity.

However, with or without these benefits, I want you to value yourself enough to be a major contributor to your own upliftment and success. Because the truth is, if you don't support yourself, no amount of external support will change your life. It may help temporarily, but without you, your transformation will have its limits.

No one else can help you, love you, or uplift you better than you can. I need you to nurture an inner environment where you feel safe and supported at all times. It won't happen overnight, and there may be times when you regress, but the sooner you start treating yourself with compassion, the sooner you will become your greatest supporter in life. Once you're there, it will become impossible to break you down. It won't matter who says what, how you mess up, or what challenges you face. If you love yourself and know your worth, nothing can stand in your way.

There is so much incredible beauty and love to behold in the world. But if your sights are set on devastation and hate, you will be blinded by it. Luckily for us all, there's a quick fix for this problem – gratitude.

THE POWER OF GRATITUDE

It's easy to have a positive outlook on life when you have a keen eye for the good things in it. Gratitude is a powerful tool to help nurture that eye. It helps you see all the things in your life that are going right rather than focusing on the things going wrong.

How you choose to see the world governs the way you *feel* in it. If you develop an eye for the good in life, you will start to see the world as a safe place and you will start to feel safer. I'm not saying you have to fool yourself about the bad things that do happen in the world. But I need you to understand that you can be aware of the bad while still focusing on the good.

But gratitude is not something you can easily flip on like a switch. It takes practice to notice things about life that you perhaps didn't see before. That is why a daily gratitude practice is one of the simplest, quickest, and most effective ways to shift your mindset in minutes. All you have to do is take five to ten minutes out of your day to write down the things you are grateful for. They can be anything from your successes in life to the great cup of coffee you just had. Big or small, everything good in your life deserves your gratitude.

Go to your Workbook now and complete the gratitude exercise waiting for you. There are enough pages there to do a week's worth of gratitude exercises. Do one now, and then commit to doing it daily from here on out. I can assure you it'll be the most rewarding 10 minutes of your day.

This gratitude exercise, along with your positive thought patterns and a solid self-care practice, will very soon turn into a positive mindset. Once you feel your mindset shift, there's no looking back. You have successfully engaged in the process of overcoming social anxiety. How do I know this? Because with a positive mindset comes confidence.

People with a positive mindset see opportunities for growth everywhere they go. They have no fear of failure because they know that every failure is an opportunity to learn something about life or themselves. Without a fear of failure, your confidence can soar. Remember what you know about confidence – it is the key to healing social anxiety.

So, if you can nurture a positive mindset, in other words, a positive lens through which you view the world and yourself, you have no reason not to have confidence. You have no reason to doubt yourself or question your worth. Not only do you have an inner

Turn Self-Doubt Into Self-Confidence

world that can successfully nurture the seed of confidence, but the way you see your outer world has shifted.

I know you might not be all the way there yet. But keep reading and hold this knowledge in your mind as we continue. Be open to the transformation process and allow yourself to relax into it. I mean, seriously, relax! If you're not sure how to let go, or even if you are, turn the page to chapter five and get ready to learn how to fully embrace this journey and have the breakthrough you're here for.

Hey, I just want you to know that I'm so proud of you. Everyone like us knows they need to make these changes but you're actually doing the work. I'm so impressed.

5

RELAX!

Your 5 Step Solution
To Solve Fight Or Flight

I'm not going to waste your time with bells and whistles. This chapter is a practical chapter. It's what you can do to actively cope with your social anxiety in your day-to-day life. It's your 5-step relaxation routine for you to do whenever you feel anxious or as a form of prevention.

You've already started to heal your social anxiety, but along your journey, you're still going to face challenges and moments of regression. That's absolutely okay! However, the more equipped you are to handle the highs and the lows, the easier it will be to recover and build your confidence.

In chapter two, you learned about the fight-or-flight response and how it forms an integral part of the anatomy of anxiety. This chapter is going to teach you how to feel safe again when it's triggered. It won't matter how much work you do on your confidence if your social anxiety is left untreated in the spur of the moment. The minute your anxiety flares up and you feel unsafe, you'll inevitably question your self-confidence again. That is why you need to be prepared. Knowing what to do during stress and anxiety will automatically increase your self-confidence and improve your coping ability.

As you now know, when your anxiety is high, it's your body responding to a perceived danger. To heal your social anxiety and stop the fight-or-flight response from happening, you need to nurture a safe inner environment. You need to prove to your mind that there is no danger, rather than getting caught in an avoidance cycle.

Healing your inner environment can take some time, but I need you ready to face your anxiety right now. That's why I want to share this 5-step fight-or-flight solution with you. You need an instant go-to when your anxiety is high. You need a relaxation routine.

Each one of these techniques is here to soothe your fight-or-flight response and help you feel safe again. Remember the affirmation from chapter two: "I am safe." Be sure to repeat that to yourself throughout this chapter as well. The techniques I will show you are some of the most powerful relaxation techniques available today. And the best part about them is you can do them at home, or anywhere else, at any time you need.

STEP 1: DEEP BREATHING

When you are in a state of anxiety, your natural fight-or-flight response is to take shorter, shallow breaths. Your heart rate also speeds up, which increases the body's need for oxygen. You might feel yourself getting breathless, lightheaded, or dizzy as a result.

But something incredible happens when you learn to control your breathing. Just as your fight-or-flight response can trigger shallow breathing and a racing heartbeat, your breathing can have an effect on your heart rate and anxiety levels in return.

When you take shallow breaths, you'll notice that your chest rises with each inhale. To consciously change your breathing pattern to have an effect on your heart rate and anxiety, you need to learn how to breathe with your diaphragm instead. This is when you breathe in and feel your stomach rise instead of your chest. These breaths are much deeper and slower than an anxious breathing pattern.

Focusing on your breathing when you're in a state of fight-or-flight can instantaneously make you feel more relaxed and slowly bring you completely down to baseline. As you deepen and slow your breathing, your body sends signals to your brain telling it that you are safe and activates your parasympathetic nervous system. You don't need to know all the fancy names for things, but what you do need to know is that your parasympathetic nervous system triggers the opposite of your fight-or-flight response. It is your body's signal to enter a state of safety and relaxation. Let's call it your rest-and-repair response.

How To Practice Deep Breathing

Deep, intentional breathing is one of the most effective ways to activate your rest-and-repair response. There are many ways you can do this, but I want to teach you three of the most effective and easy-to-remember techniques:

- **Diaphragmatic breathing:** Place one hand on your chest above your heart and the other on your upper stomach. As you breathe, I want you to pull the air down into your stomach until you feel your hand lift. You want the hand on your chest to stay completely still while the one on your stomach rises and falls with each breath. Repeat for as long as it takes to feel the powerful relaxation effects.

- **Alternate nostril breathing:** Prepare your right hand thumb and ring finger by holding your other fingers out of the way. Place your thumb on your right nostril and exhale fully through your left nostril. Keeping your thumb in place, inhale through your left nostril. Using your ring finger, block your left nostril and exhale through your right nostril. Hold your ring finger in place and inhale through your right nostril. Repeat this process, exhaling and inhaling through each nostril to help you focus on controlling your breathing in times of anxiety.

- **Square Breathing:** Combine this exercise with diaphragmatic breathing to experience the full relaxation effects. As you breathe deeply into your diaphragm, try to make your inhale and exhale of equal duration like a square with equal sides. Choose a count that feels comfortable for you to avoid light-headedness. For example, if you choose a count of five, inhale to the count of five and exhale to the count of five. Breathe in for 1, 2, 3, 4, 5, and out for 1, 2, 3, 4, 5. Repeat for as long as necessary. Often as little as five minutes is more than enough.

Let intentional deep breathing become your instinctive first response to social anxiety. It is your first step to activating your rest-and-repair response for you to feel safe again. You can repeat the affirmation, "I am safe" in your head as you breathe to set the intention for the exercise. You can also do this deep breathing while you process and reframe negative thoughts that come up.

Use it in whichever way feels the most useful for you. The more you practice deep breathing, the more it will become second nature in the face of anxiety. Don't be afraid to take a trip to the bathroom during a social event to practice your breathing. The more you treat your anxiety as it comes, the closer you'll get to feeling safe and happy in whatever social activities usually get to you.

STEP 2: MINDFULNESS MEDITATION

The fight-or-flight response, or the feeling of anxiety you get, can go one of two basic ways: Fight or flight. Fight includes a heightening of the senses, a racing heartbeat, and other bodily responses that prepare you to fight for your life. However, the opposite of that includes a sense of detachment from your body or loss of control. This is your body's way of escaping pain or trauma in the moment.

However, because there is no authentic danger to escape from, you're left feeling detached from a situation you'd rather be enjoying. Your senses feel dull, your mind retreats inward, and you suddenly don't feel comfortable in your own skin. Just like deep breathing can reverse the effects of anxiety, mindfulness exercises can reverse the flight response.

Mindfulness exercises work to bring you and all of your senses back into the present moment. Social anxiety can get into your head and make you fixate on past events that went wrong or future hypothetical events. Bringing your awareness back into the present will help ground you in the joy and fun around you instead of letting your mind slip away in fear. The more present you can be, the more open you are to reality rather than the fiction anxiety creates.

How To Practice Mindfulness

You can learn to practice mindfulness in various forms. But mindfulness meditation is, in many ways, the most effective. I want you to try it right now as you're holding this book.

- **Step 1:** Start by taking a deep breath in through your nose and slowly letting it out through your mouth. Make sure it is a diaphragmatic breath like you've now learned. Continue to breathe with intention throughout this exercise. As you breathe, take a moment to check in with each of your senses. Your five senses are what keep you grounded in physical reality.

- **Step 2:** Start with your sense of sight. Take in the details of the world around you. What can you see? Name 5 things right now. How much of the color red is around you? How about blue? Any details that you can take in with your eyes will do.

- **Step 3:** Next, tune in to your sense of hearing. Maybe you can hear your deep breaths releasing from your mouth. Maybe there are birds in the background, the sound of traffic, or whatever sounds you can hear in your environment right now. Bring your awareness to each one for a moment.

- **Step 4:** Now, I want you to pay attention to your sense of touch. Pick up any smaller object around you. What sensations do you notice about it? How heavy is it on your wrist? What textures can you feel with your fingertips? Notice the sensations of your body where you're sitting right now. What are the textures of the sofa, chair, or bed you're relaxing on? Are they soft, rough, furry, or slick? Can you feel the air against your face? Bring your awareness to each and everything you can feel with your body right now.

- **Step 5:** Your sight, sound, and touch are the three most essential senses for you to use during this exercise because they are the easiest to tune into no matter what you're doing. But, to make the most of this experience, I want you to grab something quick to eat or drink. Before you take a bite or sip of whatever you've chosen, I want you to smell it. Pay attention to the different aromas you can smell. Now take a bite or sip and savor it for a moment. What do you taste? Are there sweetness, bitterness, or savory flavors? Allow your sense of smell and taste to work together in this experience. Take it all in like it's the first time trying it.

- **Step 6:** You've successfully grounded yourself using your five senses! Continue reading the words on these pages and pay attention to how you feel. Do you feel more relaxed, centered, and immersed in this moment? That's the power of mindfulness meditation.

Just like deep breathing, you can also practice mindfulness meditation anywhere you go. All you need is a few moments to yourself to restore your senses to the present. You can implement mindfulness into waking social moments by simply focusing on each of your senses as you talk or listen.

If you feel yourself becoming overwhelmed by anxiety but aren't able to get up and escape the situation for a moment, simply follow the steps above without changing a thing. You might get too distracted by this at first, but the more you practice mindfulness, the quicker and easier this will become. The focus is to ground your senses into the present moment, even if that present moment is having a conversation in a public coffee shop.

STEP 3: VISUALIZATION

By now, I'm sure you know that your mind is your most powerful tool for overcoming any struggle and living a fulfilling life. Your mind is full of surprising abilities and strengths. One of those strengths is visualization. This is when your mind uses your imagination to allow you to experience things before they happen. Your mind can trick your body in almost every way into believing it is experiencing something it's not.

Just like your mind can catastrophize a social scenario to make you enter the fight-or-flight state, it is just as capable of visualizing such a safe environment that it triggers your body's rest-and-repair response. The only difference between the two is which way your mind chooses to go. Are you going to envision the worst of the worst? Or are you ready to harness the power of your mind to make you feel safe in the darkest of times?

Part of social anxiety is the anticipation you feel before an event or meet up. This is because catastrophizing the outcome of the situation is your anxiety's natural instinct. You want to feel as prepared as possible for things that could go wrong. But, visualization is all about preparing yourself for when things go right. Instead of triggering your anxiety over hypothetical problems, I want you to start triggering your excitement for hypothetical moments of connection and fun.

The more time you spend thinking about negative outcomes, the more you make catastrophizing a habit and in many ways create negative outcomes. But if you intentionally spend time visualizing the best outcome of a social situation, it's more likely you will form a *positive* habit around your thinking and create a positive outcome.

How To Visualize Yourself To Social Safety

There are a few ways that you can use visualization to heal from social anxiety. You can use it to increase your relaxation in times of stress, and you can use it to form a positive attitude around socializing.

To start out with any visualization method I recommend finding a quiet place, making yourself comfortable, closing your eyes, and using diaphragmatic breathing to help you focus. Use your imagination to bring up images and shift the images in a way that is beneficial. Let me break down some visualization techniques for you:

- **Anxiety relief visualization:** This visualization is a healthy way for you to detach from a stressful situation and help yourself feel safe again. It is a way for you to "go to a happier place" when you feel stuck in a state of anxiety. Once you're ready, start to visualize somewhere you normally feel at peace. This can be anywhere from the beach, a forest, a wide open green field, or even a place in your home.

  Visualize yourself in this special place and allow yourself to become fully immersed in the environment. Use your senses to help you embrace the visualization process. In your mind's eye, or imagination, try to look around the space and take in the details. Look around for what you can see, imagine the feeling of being in this space, imagine a comforting smell, and listen for any sounds that you "hear" in this space. Feel the emotions that come up while you're here and allow them to replace your anxiety. Feel the peace, the tranquility, and the comfort this place brings.

Use this technique whenever you are in a state of anxiety and need to mentally escape for a moment to calm yourself.

- **Positive social revisualization:** This visualization technique is all about nurturing a positive outlook on social environments. This is how you can kick catastrophizing to the curb and turn your anxiety into genuine excitement. You would normally use this visualization before a social event or meeting you already have planned. Instead of worrying about the worst-case scenario, you reprogram your thinking to anticipate a good time.

    When you are ready, start the visualization by imagining yourself at the social event you have planned. Allow your mind to go wild and imagine the best possible outcome for the event. Even if the visualization seems a little over the top, the following emotions will be far more positive than if you had imagined the worst-case scenario. It's okay to get a little silly with the visualization to help you spark joy and laughter about the event.

    You can also use this visualization technique to practice social events before they happen. Having a chance to "live" the experience in your mind before it happens can help you feel more confident in the moment. You would have already played out a good evening in your head, taking the pressure off of the need to anticipate how it'll go.

Of course, this exercise is not about creating unrealistic expectations but rather getting into the habit of seeing social events in a more positive light to break the habit of catastrophizing.

- **Self-discovery visualization:** This type of visualization helps you to figure out what kinds of social interactions feel good for you. I want you to imagine yourself in an uncomfortable social setting you've been through before. Play out the memory in your head, but this time visualize the outcome you would have preferred.

    Compare the two scenarios in your head and use the comparison to help you discover what you do and don't like in social situations. Knowing your boundaries and understanding where you might go wrong sometimes can help you feel more prepared and, therefore, more confident in future social engagements.

    You can do this visualization at any time by just imagining a social interaction you often have to engage in and visualizing the outcome that you hope to experience. Allow the visualization to unfold, and pay attention to the details that stand out to you.

Visualization might feel difficult at first, especially if you aren't used to imagining things in your head in image form. However, with time and practice, your visualizations will become far more vivid and automatic.

Your mind is like a muscle. The more you do a certain thing, the stronger it becomes. The power of your mind is the same reason social anxiety can have such a major impact on your life. So, why not harness that power and use it for good rather than allowing anxiety to use it against you?

STEP 4: PROGRESSIVE MUSCLE RELAXATION

If deep breathing is the foundation for a successful relaxation routine, and harnessing the power of your mind through mindfulness and visualization comes next, then the logical progression to your routine is releasing energy and tension in the body. The body is just as important as the mind in anxiety relief.

Stress and anxiety can create a lot of tension in the body, making muscles seize up and become tight. Every mechanism in the body works together, so just like breathing deeply can reverse a fight-or-flight response, easing the tension in your body caused by anxiety can help your mind relax as well.

One of the most profound ways that you can release tension in the body to induce a relaxed state is with progressive muscle relaxation (PMR). Even though PMR is a fantastic way to feel the anxiety melt out of your muscles, the method is unexpected. Instead of purposefully relaxing each muscle in the body, the method involves tensing them. In this case, fighting fire with fireworks!

Progressive muscle relaxation can not only decrease anxiety, but it can help to relieve a variety of tension-related problems. It can improve back and neck pain, help with migraines, and help you get a better night's sleep – all things that will contribute to a relaxed state of being.

How To Use Muscle Relaxation To Heal

Just like many of the other exercises in your relaxation routine, you want to try this method when you have a moment to yourself in a quiet, comfortable place. If you wear glasses or contacts, it's better to remove them for this process. Wearing loose-fitting clothes is also recommended.

- Lying down in a comfortable place like on your sofa or bed, start the exercise with deep diaphragmatic breathing. A couple of deep breaths will do. Just use your breath to relax into the exercise and get started.

- Starting with your forehead, tense all the muscles as hard and steady as you can for 15 seconds. Feel the tension and be prepared to notice the incredible difference. When the 15 seconds are up, release the tension and relax your forehead muscles for 30 seconds. Remember to breathe throughout this process. Do not hold your breath at any stage.

- Clench your jaw and hold for 15 seconds, making sure not to put too much pressure on your teeth. Then, relax for 30 seconds.

- Next, go to your neck and shoulders. Scrunch your shoulders up to your ears and squeeze for 15 seconds before relaxing for 30.

- Take your hands and ball them into tight fists. Push your fists into your chest for 15 seconds and release for another 30.

- Repeat the process with each major muscle group in the body, including the bum, legs, calves, and feet.

- Allow yourself to rest for a moment before getting up. If you fall asleep, take that as a sign that you did a great job!

Pay attention to the instant relaxation this exercise creates in the body and mind. It only takes fifteen minutes, more or less, to complete, and it doesn't take much mental legwork to get right. The process is all in the body, yet it has a profoundly positive impact on the mind. PMR is one of the best ways to release trapped tension caused by anxiety. You can do it every night before going to bed or whenever you need to let go of tension.

STEP 5: SELF-CARE PRACTICES

We already discussed the importance of self-care in Chapter 4, but I want it to be part of your regular relaxation routine. In some way, each of the exercises listed above form part of a self-care practice. But the self-care activities you love to do deserve to be acknowledged here.

Self-care is one of the ways that you can maintain a healthy body, mind, and soul by taking time out of every day to look after yourself properly. A good self-care practice can improve overall well-being, decrease anxiety, and help you feel loved and supported by yourself and others.

How To Love And Care For Yourself Correctly

There are limitless ways to love and care for yourself but sometimes it's easy to forget what works for you. Your well-being is built on the various elements of health. These include:

- **Physical:** Physical self-care is anything that contributes to a healthy body. It includes hygiene practices, eating nutritious foods, exercising regularly, and taking care of your external appearance.

- **Emotional:** Emotional self-care is anything you do to nurture your emotional well-being. It can include listening to uplifting music, watching a comedy show, releasing unwanted emotions, and anything else that improves your emotional state in a healthy way.

- **Mental:** Mental self-care includes activities that fulfill your mental need for stimulation. It can include spending time learning a new skill, reading a book, working on a project, and any other form of healthy mental stimulation.

- **Social:** I'm sure you know all about what social self-care means. Social anxiety is one of the greatest killers of social health. Self-care activities that improve social health include spending time with a close friend, calling someone you love in times of need, joining online forums of like-minded people, and so much more.

- **Spiritual:** Spiritual self-care includes anything that helps you feel more connected to your spiritual self. This will look different for everyone depending on your beliefs. But some activities can include spending time in nature, connecting with animals, reading religious scriptures, or other spiritual wisdom.

You can use whichever forms of self-care work best for you. Try to implement at least one self-care practice from each of these elements of well-being per day. You are a complex being made up of multifaceted needs. Honor yourself and take care of yourself the way you know is best.

I am so proud of you for getting to this point in your journey. You have learned the foundation for a successful social anxiety recovery. From chapter one to now, you've learned and implemented so many powerful tools to solve this problem. Your inner world is becoming the safe space you need it to be, and your mindset is thriving. Now, take what you've learned, and continue to practice it regularly. Don't give up or get slack on these techniques. If you forget, go to your Workbook and review your relaxation routine on the pages there.

I want you to keep growing and I want your confidence to surprise you and everyone you know in the best way. So keep up with what you've been doing since chapter one and turn to the next book. The next step along your journey is to get educated on the skills it takes to become the social butterfly you've always been on the inside.

BOOK 2

SOCIAL SKILLS

1 **From Awkward To Awesome
   Through Better Communication**   102
   The NASA Formula For Enhanced
   Social Confidence

2 **The Butterfly Emerges**   123
   5 Strategies For Rapid Success

3 **From Fear To Fun With Gradual Exposure**   152
   Subtitle: Steps For Reclaiming Control
   Over Anxiety Triggers

4 **Skip Over The Usual Social Hurdles**   178
   How Self-Compassion And Understanding
   Create Social Comfort

5 **Staying On Track & Staying Social**   196
   How To Integrate This New Freedom
   Into Your Life, Forever

FROM AWKWARD TO AWESOME THROUGH BETTER COMMUNICATION

The NASA Formula For Enhanced Social Confidence

Like a lemon seed in the soil, a lotus in the muck, or a caterpillar turned to mush inside its cocoon, the first half of this book has been about going within yourself and understanding your social anxiety.

You had to work on your inner environment, overcome negative thought patterns, start building your self-confidence, and more. Now, you're almost ready for the full social butterfly transformation! But before you sprout, bloom, or fly, there's something important I need to tell you – your communication needs work.

Without good communication skills, social interaction can become awkward. This book contains the essential concepts and techniques to eradicate social anxiety for good. But just like the lotus has to bud before it blooms, the caterpillar cocoons before it flies, and the seed has to sprout and grow before it becomes a tree, building communication skills is the interim stage you have to master before taking the fantastic final steps that await you.

Skillful communication will bind together each technique you learn from chapters 2 to 5 of this book and help you succeed in every way. In this chapter, I'm going to show you how to go from awkward to awesome in no time at all. You can't go any further along your healing journey if you don't spend some time learning better communication skills. Communication skills are going to be your backbone in every social interaction you have. Improve them, and your confidence will soar.

Anxiety has a way of squashing communication skills. It tears your eye contact away in fear, hunches your shoulders in shame, and stammers your speech in trepidation. Over time, when you've had some form of recurring anxiety like social anxiety, this awkwardness becomes your default. But it doesn't have to be permanent. You can reclaim your confidence by learning, or relearning, good communication skills.

Remember how important confidence is to healing social anxiety? It's safe to say that it's the cure. This is yet another way that you can improve your confidence. If you have good communication skills, you will feel more equipped to handle any kind of conversation that you enter into. You'll have a better idea of when to say what, how to act, and the other person's feelings. The main difference between awkwardness and awesomeness is communication skill.

But don't worry; the best part about this step is that it comes down to a very simple formula. I call it NASA. No, not NASA the space organization, but NASA, as in an enneagram for the four aspects of good communication: Nonverbal communication, active listening, speaking effectively, and assertiveness. If you can master these, you'll be a supernova – unstoppable.

THE FOUR ASPECTS OF GOOD COMMUNICATION

I'm going to get straight into the details so you can move on to the next four chapters of this book and kiss social anxiety goodbye for good. This formula is the glue that will hold everything you learned in previous chapters and everything you're about to learn together in one congruent skillset. The four aspects of good communication are:

NASA!

- **Nonverbal communication:** Using body language, tone of voice, and facial expressions to communicate in a confident and appealing way.

- **Active listening:** The ability to actively listen to and engage with another person in conversation.

- **Speaking effectively:** Speaking in a clear and confident manner to get your points across effectively.

- **Assertiveness:** Stating your boundaries and needs without being too aggressive or passive.

I want you to use NASA to help remind you of these four vital communication skills. If you can remember to do these four things, your social life will blossom from here. But of course, there's more to NASA than simply remembering the meaning. You have to put each of these four communication skills to good practice. Let me break them down for you:

Nonverbal Communication

The funny thing about communication is that over 90%[4] of it is nonverbal. That means that we communicate without our words most of the time. Without good nonverbal communication skills, you can say all the right things and still be awkward. Let me paint a picture for you.

Imagine you go out for dinner and you see a young man making a move on a woman. He could be the nicest, most well-worded guy giving all the right compliments to her, but if his posture is slouched, his smile is too intense, and he's holding his hands politely behind his back as he trips over his words, the last thing he's conveying is confidence. It's okay if you cringed at that!

Now imagine the same young man walking over to the same woman and introducing himself in a smooth tone of voice. This time he sits down at her table, puts his hands together in front of him and leans forward slightly. He smiles softly and makes gentle eye contact as he gives her a compliment. See the difference?

Nonverbal communication is one of the reasons why some people seem to be so popular and attractive no matter how they look or what they say. They simply ooze confidence and likeability. That essence they give off that makes you want to be around them is a strong nonverbal communication skill.

Bad nonverbal communication can look like:

- Bad posture
- Uninterested facial expression
- Excessive fidgeting
- Folded arms
- Avoiding eye contact
- Too much eye contact
- Excessive sighing
- Sarcastic tone of voice
- Nervousness
- Talking too fast or too slow

Bad nonverbal communication sends the wrong message. It tells other people that you don't want to be there and you aren't comfortable. It can also send a false message and make someone think you don't like them when you do.

Whatever your nonverbal communication looks like now, if you want to become the person that everyone enjoys talking to, start by sending the right message non-verbally.

Good nonverbal communication can look like:

- Relaxed and comfortable facial expressions
- Appropriate smiling
- Confident and open body posture
- Pleasant tone of voice
- Appropriate eye-contact
- Leaning in towards others
- Friendly nudges or touching

It's amazing how many ways we can communicate without saying a word. Good nonverbal communication can take your social confidence to the next level very quickly. It won't be hard for people to enjoy your company, and you're far more likely to feel more comfortable yourself. But, if you're unlearning bad nonverbal communication, practice is essential.

Practicing good nonverbal communication will teach you a lot. As you implement new strategies into your communication style, you'll quickly notice how people change in response to you. But before you take your nonverbal communication skills into the real world, I want you to go to your Workbook right now and do the practice exercise waiting for you. You're going to have a pretend conversation with yourself in the mirror. There are extra prompts in your Workbook and space for your notes.

I want you to stand in front of the mirror and imagine someone has asked you a question. Now, enact how you would respond. Analyze your facial expression and ask yourself what message it is giving across. Do you look intrigued to have been asked a question, or irritated? Write down what you see. Try it again but this time pretend someone has just told you something sad that has happened to them. Enact how you would naturally respond and analyze your facial expressions. Do you look empathetic and caring, or do you come across as uninterested? Again, write it down.

If your nonverbal communication isn't sending the message you want it to, experiment with yourself in the mirror and try out different ways to respond. Maybe add in a gentle arm touch when someone tells you something sad, or raise your eyebrows slightly to seem more interested depending on the context. If you can be overly expressive, like I know I am, some situations might require you to take it down a notch. This can include lowering the volume of your voice, holding back arm gestures a bit, softening your smile, and any subtle reduction in nonverbal communication.

I'm not telling you to become someone you're not but be realistic with what you see in the mirror. You might be more or less expressive than you realize. Remember, communication is about translating how you feel and what you want to say to the other person accurately. If your nonverbal communication is coming on too strong or not strong enough, your amazing personality may get lost in translation.

Use the list of positive nonverbal cues to help you out and see how your face and body language can change in the mirror with such little effort. Play around with this exercise and have fun with it! Allow yourself to see the silliness in human nonverbal communication and know that it's a system you can hack.

Nonverbal communication is something you can practice and improve on with time. Once you are aware of your usual nonverbal communication signals, you will start to know yourself better and know which situations require a little bit more effort and self-awareness.

When you're ready, take your improved skill and put it to the test. Pay attention to how people respond to you when you make more effort or take it down a notch. The better people are responding to you, the more likely it is that you're giving the right nonverbal message.

Active Listening

There's more to listening than hearing the words coming out of a person's mouth. To listen, I mean truly *listen*, you have to become an active listener. This means showing the other person that you are interested in what they're saying and that you've been paying attention. But how do you show someone something that's invisible?

Good communication skills are about making the other person feel comfortable speaking to you rather than how well you are taking in the conversation. You could be listening to every word that someone says while making them feel awkward and unheard. That defeats the point of social connection.

The trick to good listening skills is making sure the other person knows they have your undivided attention. This is where you can use nonverbal communication to your advantage among other techniques. Active listening can include:

- Allowing the other person to get enough chances to talk.
- Asking questions related to what the person is saying.
- Giving genuine responses to specific things they are talking about.
- Using nonverbal communication to show that you're engaged.

It can take some practice, but if you focus on how you are making the other person feel, you'll be more likely to step into your empathy and actively listen to whoever you're talking to. Good listening is about the other person. It's about empathy and a desire to learn or understand something about them. Active listening can also help shift the focus of the conversation onto the other person and reduce anxious thoughts about yourself.

Let me repeat that: <u>Active listening can reduce anxiety by taking your attention away from yourself.</u>

If you struggle with empathy, you can also allow your curiosity to pull you through conversation. When you are genuinely curious about what the person is going to say next, you'll have an easier time listening to them.

I want you to try something the next time you're in conversation with someone you really enjoy being around. Maybe they're someone who makes you feel heard and understood. Maybe they are a great listener and that's one of the reasons you feel you can open up to them. Either way, the next time you see them, I want you to look for active signs of listening in them. Are they nodding their head as you speak and appearing interested in what you say? Are they asking you questions like "And then what happened?" to encourage you to keep talking? Or are they giving very specific responses to certain things you're saying? But, most of all, how are they making you feel? If you feel heard, understood, and comfortable talking, they are a good active listener.

Once you know what good listening is, it's easier to identify and replicate it yourself. You'd be surprised how much you can learn by observing other people in conversation. If you enjoy someone's company, try to identify signs of good listening and practice actively listening in return.

For example, instead of sitting with your arms folded and your eyes dancing around the room, try to lean forward a little bit, nod your head occasionally to show that you're understanding what's being said, and make sure to smile or laugh if the person makes a humorous remark. Ask questions related to what the person is saying, or reply with your genuine thoughts and feelings. Try to make eye contact in a way that's comfortable for you – a little bit can go a long way.

A great indication that you are showing good listening skills is if the person you are talking to becomes comfortable prolonging the conversation or sharing more personal details about themselves and their lives.

Remember, the more you focus on showing empathy for the person you're speaking with, the less you'll be in your head with anxious thoughts, and the more you will both enjoy the conversation.

Speaking Effectively

Effective speaking is the ability to use your words to communicate as clearly and concisely as possible. This comes from effective thinking. Both require clarity and precision, but you can't have one without the other. When you are confident about what you want to say and how you will say it, speaking effectively becomes a breeze.

One of the first things to go out the door when social anxiety hits is your speaking. This is because anxiety consumes your thoughts. The great news here is you already know how to keep your thoughts in check.

The more you can pull your mind out of a negative thought spiral and reinforce coherent thinking patterns, the sooner your words will comfortably start to flow again in conversation. In other words, you have to get out of your head in order to speak up.

Anxiety can cause inefficient speaking very easily. That can look like:

- Speaking too quickly or slowly.
- Stumbling over your words.
- Using too many filler words, like "um" and "ah."
- Freezing up and saying nothing.
- Saying things you don't mean.
- Interjecting what you want to say at the wrong time.
- Stuttering or speech impediments.

Once you can catch yourself speaking inefficiently, check in with your thoughts. Use your ability to be a conscious observer of your thoughts, as you learned in Chapter 3 of Book 1.

Observing your thoughts when you aren't speaking clearly will likely reveal various negative thinking patterns, such as racing thoughts, catastrophizing, and general negative thinking. Once your thoughts are under control, you should notice yourself speaking more effectively.

Effective speaking can look like:

- Clear enunciation of words.
- Concise points that are easily absorbed by others.
- Appropriate speaking speed.
- Appropriate speaking volume.
- Confident nonverbal communication.

Now that you know what effective speaking is, you can actively practice speaking in a more effective way. Maybe at first, you might continue to mess up and seem awkward, but as your confidence grows, your speaking will improve.

Remember, true confidence is when you genuinely don't care about making mistakes in front of others. When you can do that, it won't matter if you stutter or stumble over your words occasionally; you can simply laugh it off and keep talking.

Confident people don't take themselves too seriously, and they have the ability to laugh at themselves. Social anxiety can catastrophize any mistake to seem like a much bigger deal than it really is. But the truth is, everyone, even people without social anxiety, stumble over their words occasionally. Most people can be distracted, anxious about something else, or even enjoying the conversation so much that they talk way too fast. That is totally normal!

Effective speaking is a great communication skill to have, but you should know that most social interaction is there for you to enjoy, and mistakes shouldn't get in the way of that. If you find yourself struggling in conversation, take a moment to breathe, observe your thoughts, and make sure they aren't putting a damper on an otherwise smooth conversation. Ease up on yourself and try to lighten up your thoughts in order to feel more confident and relaxed.

Assertiveness

Arguably, the toughest thing to master when you have anxiety of any kind is becoming more assertive. Assertiveness is not the same as being aggressive. It is about stating your boundaries and needs in a way that is clear and serious without being negative.

The opposite of being assertive is being passive. It may sound good to be passive to avoid conflict with other people, but being too passive can cause you to have your needs unmet and boundaries overstepped. If you are not assertive enough, you may bottle up your feelings and eventually explode when you are pushed to your limit. You might also become self-destructive in an attempt to cope with the built-up emotions.

Assertiveness will give you the opportunity to let people know how you need to be treated in order to be comfortable so that others can respect you and understand you better.

Everyone is unique, and everyone has unique boundaries. Without stating what your boundaries are, you leave yourself open to having them crossed and eventually creating conflict for yourself. Becoming more assertive will naturally show people that you are confident and that you care about yourself. This is a great way to harbor respect and rapport. Assertiveness can look like:

- Clearly stating a need or boundary in a straightforward manner.
- Apologizing only when necessary instead of excessively saying "sorry."
- Using confident body language and tone when speaking.
- Addressing problems directly without getting aggressive.

A lack of proper assertiveness is a sign that you are holding onto false beliefs about yourself and others. For example, if you don't feel like you are worthy enough, you won't stand up for yourself because you won't believe that you deserve better treatment. You will likely have a habit of being too passive. Or, if you believe that people are inherently untrustworthy and out to get you, you will likely become aggressive at the first sign of conflict against your boundaries or needs. Either way, it's okay because, as you know, false beliefs can be healed.

However, while you're healing and working on your false beliefs, using the methods you learned in chapters 3 and 4, Book 1. You can start practicing assertiveness right now. I want you to go to your Workbook now and write down what your needs and boundaries in social situations are.

I want you to write down things that you enjoy in social settings, such as long hugs from friends, lots of joking and laughter, a safe space to share and be vulnerable, or acceptance. These are your needs. They are the things that make you feel fulfilled in a social environment.

Then, I want you to write down things you don't enjoy in social settings such as being hugged by strangers, being touched too much, intense long-held eye-contact, name-calling or swearing, being interrupted, or being called certain pet names. These are your boundaries. They are the things that make you feel uncomfortable or disrespected in a social environment.

Now that you know what your needs and boundaries are, I want you to practice saying them out loud. You can start by using your mirror like you did while learning better nonverbal communication.

Then, when you're ready, start sharing your needs and boundaries with others in an assertive way. This can sound like:

- "Hey, I know you think that pet name is cute, but I would prefer you didn't use it for me."

- "Thank you for being so caring, but I don't like to be hugged so tightly."

- "I really like it when you watch my football games, Dad. Please come more often."

- "James, I know you like cars, but can we discuss topics that we're both interested in today?"

- "I love long hugs, feel free to drag them out, Mom!"

- "Sarah, I'm not okay with being called names. Please never call me that again."

- "I don't like big crowds, I'd prefer if we spent time together out in nature next time."

Can you see how none of these statements are offensive in any way? They are straightforward and clear. The person you're speaking to shouldn't have to wonder what you are asking of them, your needs and boundaries must be communicated clearly in an assertive tone. If your assertiveness creates conflict between you and another person, I need you to know that it is likely a "them" problem and not a "you" problem. Some people will not respect your needs or boundaries, and they are not the kind of people you need to worry about socializing with, at least not too often.

The right people who deserve to be in your life will listen and understand, even if they don't agree or like what you're saying. You are worthy of having your needs and boundaries respected, and the only people worthy of your time and energy are those who will listen when you're assertive instead of denying your needs.

You can use NASA as a universal strategy for almost any social situation. Once these basic communication skills are in place, your confidence will already be at a level where engaging with people in situations that would normally make you feel anxious feels easy.

Some areas where you can use NASA to improve your social rapport and gain confidence include:

- Your friendships
- Your relationships
- Your family time
- Your professional life
- Your parenting
- Your leisure time

Different social settings come with different potential problems, all of which can be improved with NASA.

BUILDING RELATIONSHIPS WITH BETTER COMMUNICATION

What are friends for but to be there for each other? When you have good communication skills, you are better equipped to show up in any relationship you have. You will be able to get out of your head and show compassion for people in times of need. You will be a more supportive friend that people can rely on. And, you will become someone that people enjoy having around.

But there is more to relationships of any kind than simple conversation, emotional support, and fun. Sometimes things go wrong, and that's where anxiety can get the better of almost anyone. Conflict is a real and often unavoidable aspect of any relationship. However, the better you can deal with conflict effectively, the less likely conflict will cause permanent damage.

Proper conflict resolution can save a relationship that is otherwise good. It can help you prolong your relationships with people and help you build life-long connections. If you can make it through the highs and the lows of relationships, be it friendships, parental, or romantic, you will break through superficial barriers and form much deeper connections in life.

There isn't some special hidden knowledge you don't know yet that will help you conquer conflict. You've already learned the way in this chapter – NASA. You can use the four communication skills to get through conflict unscathed and possibly better off. If you can:

- **Nonverbal communication:** Be aware of what your nonverbal communication is conveying to the other person and adjust it to show that you are not being aggressive, but rather that you care and are open to talk.

- **Active listening:** Use conflict as a chance to truly listen to the other person and show empathy. Remember, active listening is about wanting to hear what the other person is really saying rather than just hearing their words and waiting for your chance to respond. It is about making the other person feel heard.

- **Speaking effectively:** Observe your thoughts for any negative thought patterns and make sure to correct them or let them go before responding. Once your thoughts are clear, you will be able to speak your true feelings more effectively.

- **Assertiveness:** Don't be afraid to be assertive of your needs and boundaries. Show that you have respect for yourself. Then, be open to listening to the other person asserting their needs and boundaries in return. Try to remind yourself that you are worthy of having your boundaries adhered to. If you become aggressive in any way or passive to asserting yourself, take it as a lesson that you have some unresolved false beliefs that you need to address and work on after the conflict is resolved.

PROFESSIONAL COMMUNICATION SKILLS

Professionalism requires some degree of confidence for you to be taken seriously in the workforce. Social anxiety can negatively impact your career and hold you back from achieving your goals. Better communication skills can improve your presence in interviews and meetings, as well as improve colleague relationships.

I want you to think about the last time you had a conversation with your employer if you are employed. If you're not employed, think about the last time you went for a job interview. How did the conversation go?

If your palms were sweating while you frantically explained something, or you felt your heart race as you anticipated a negative remark, anxiety has likely held you back from success in your professional field.

Good professional connections are a very big part of any successful business. Improving your communication skills can have a ripple effect on things you never expected, such as finances.

From here on out, I want you to use NASA to help you succeed in your professional life. This could look like:

- **Nonverbal communication:** When giving a presentation, stand up straight, keep your arms open and relaxed, and make sure you are using facial expressions that keep the room intrigued. If you don't look confident in what you're saying, other people won't be confident in your ideas.

- **Active listening:** In a meeting, lean forward slightly with your hands together on the table in front of you and nod your head occasionally to show that you are engaged and interested in what is being said.

- **Speaking effectively:** Make sure your thoughts are clear and concise before you open your mouth to speak. If you are distracted or unsure about how to make your points in a meeting or interview there is more chance of them coming out wrong or making you sound unprepared.

- **Assertiveness:** if a colleague is negatively impacting your workspace, use assertiveness to state your boundaries without causing unnecessary conflict. You can also use assertiveness to state your needs to a potential employer during an interview. The more confident you are, the more likely they will consider your proposition.

Building your communication skills is how you can take your positive internal environment and start putting it into practice. The way that you communicate reveals how confident you are in yourself and how high your self-esteem is. But, the funny thing is, when you practice NASA, it will reveal the confidence and self-worth you didn't know you had.

I want you to use this strategy alongside the effort you are continually making to improve your inner environment. I want you to continue to work on yourself as we move forward and tackle the exciting practices coming up in chapters 2 - 5.

Everything you do throughout this book compliments and builds on each other. No cog in this system for fighting social anxiety is there in vain. Take each one seriously, and don't give up on any of them. Trust the process, and keep doing your inner work as you emerge from your cocoon and become the social butterfly we both know you are. Turn the page now and get ready to fly.

2

THE BUTTERFLY EMERGES

5 Strategies For Rapid Success

There was a time in my life when my anxiety was so in control that it stopped me from leaving the house at all. I stopped seeing friends, I stopped doing the things I loved doing, and I allowed anxiety to become who I was. Like a hermit crab refusing to leave its shell, I was stubbornly trapped in my head.

The truth is, I didn't want to be trapped anymore, but I was too scared to take the leap and do the things that I knew I needed to do to get better. I was afraid of the possibilities of what would become of me – I was afraid of the unknown. That's what this chapter is all about. Facing the unknown and embracing the outcomes, whatever they may be.

Everything you've learned until this point has required some form of bravery. You've had to accept discomfort and face parts of yourself that are difficult to face. You've had to face the pain of what you've been missing out on to find the passion to make a change. And you've had to open your mind and try new things in your pursuit of social happiness. But these next two chapters will require all the bravery you've got. Are you ready?

It doesn't matter how you answered that question. No matter how scared you are to move into this practical, real-world, social-exposure phase, I need you to be brave and move forward anyway. This chapter, and the next one, include all the things that I was too afraid to do for years of my life. It includes the things that eventually saved me from the painful shell I was outgrowing.

As a hermit, convinced that my tiny shell was the only safety I'd ever know, I was wrong. It was crushing me.

Along with what you've already learned up until this point, everything I'm about to teach you ripped my shell wide open and allowed me to realize that I wasn't a hermit crab after all, I was a social butterfly. I just needed to push myself into the unknown and find the freedom waiting for me there.

I KNOW that you are a social butterfly too. It's only a matter of emerging from your shell and finding your wings to fly. Anxiety has hidden your potential from you, but it's always been there. In this chapter, I want you to have an open mind and be willing to try something that scares you. You must be willing to leap into the unknown and trust that you will find your safety again.

I know by now your confidence has improved since page one. But it's about to get even stronger. You'll need the NASA communication skill strategy from Chapter 1, so keep it in mind as we get started on the next big cog in your social success system: Social skills.

Building social skills is not something that you can learn in a book. At least not all the way. You can learn them theoretically, but true social skills can only be learned in practice. Your social skills revolve around your ability to adapt and thrive in a variety of social situations. But you can only see a true improvement in social skills by practicing strategies for social success in real life.

Don't let that scare you just yet. This chapter is not here to push you off the edge and say, "Good luck!" It's here to help prepare you for the biggest step you'll take along your journey – turning fear into fun with gradual exposure, which you will learn in the next chapter.

Gradual exposure is the epitome of social anxiety treatment. It's going to build your confidence faster than anything else can, and you know what that means – Goodbye social anxiety! But gradual exposure can feel like too big a hurdle to try just yet. And that's why you need to know these 5 strategies for building social skills first.

STEP 1: BREAK THE AVOIDANCE CYCLE

Think of this step as dipping your toe into the water before diving in. To start building self-confidence that will last for the long term, you have to break the avoidance cycle. In Chapter 2, Book 1, we went into depth about the avoidance cycle and how it creates a snowball effect for worsening anxiety. But just think about it: how can you improve your anxiety before you stop it from getting worse? You can't.

So, the first step you have to take to overcome your anxiety and build social skills is to break the avoidance cycle you're stuck in. And there's only one surefire way you can do that: do something that scares you!

I don't mean that you need to do something dangerous. But I need you to start doing things that your brain **perceives** as dangerous in order to prove to yourself that you are safe. That's the gist of exposure therapy – exposing yourself to situations that trigger your anxiety to help you overcome your fear. It is the direct act of facing your fears. Now is the time I need you to do that. I need you to decide right now that you're not going to let your anxiety hold you back.

You should know that deciding this isn't going to magically erase your anxiety, but it IS putting you back in control of how you live your life. Anxiety may still plague every social situation you encounter for a while. But by the end of this book, you will have had enough practice living life to your fullest potential regardless of the anxiety that it will begin to melt away. And it all starts here. It all starts with your choice to break the avoidance cycle.

I want you to remember what I told you in Chapter 2, Book 1: Words have power. Your words will help you summon up the bravery you need to go through with this step. You can use mantras to keep your mind focused and feeling safe. This is when I recommend using the "I am safe" mantra to remind yourself that everything is fine. It's only your anxiety playing up.

You can also use the positive thinking techniques from Chapter 3, Book 1, to help you redirect your thinking patterns while tackling a scary social interaction. Then, if you feel yourself going into fight-or-flight mode as you anticipate disaster, refer back to what you learned in Chapter 5, Book 1, about solving fight-or-flight.

You see, everything you've learned so far was setting you up for this moment right now. You are ready for this, I promise.

This chapter is preparing you for the in-person activities you will actively try in Chapter 3. So for step one, the first strategy for social success, you're simply going to decide. You've had enough of letting anxiety rule your life and this is where that ends. Make a choice right now, and keep that commitment to yourself from here on out. Make yourself a promise that even though you might be experiencing anxiety, you're not going to let it stand in your way. You have the tools to fight it, so choose to fight.

Now that you've decided, go out into the world and slowly allow yourself more freedom. Instead of being stuck in an avoidance cycle, where your anxiety snowballs into a mess of missing out, I want you to get stuck in an acceptance cycle, where your positive experiences from letting go of fear snowball into a reduction in anxiety.

Don't put too much pressure on yourself just yet. There's more to exposure therapy than just doing things that scare you. But we'll get into that in more detail in Chapter 3.

However, until you get there, I want you to feel the sensation of freeing yourself start to bubble up from within. Your choice is about to make waves in your life and you're a chapter away from taking everything you're learning and applying it. Don't look back. Keep reading.

STEP 2: START A CONVERSATION

The choice is made. It's done! You're officially moving forward and emerging from the shell of anxiety you've had shrouded over you. Now you need some useful tips to help you feel confident out in the real world.

I don't want you to finish this book feeling like you can only just make it through a night out with your friends or a dinner with your family. I want you to close this book at the end of Chapter 5 and feel excited to build connections, live your life, and have fun!

These next four tips are the strategies you need to emerge with confidence and swiftly tackle the currents of socializing.

Socializing is never smooth sailing 100% of the time – anxiety or not. But if you have the tools to stay above awkward moments and negativity, along with the social skills to intrigue others, stay energized, and find joy in talking to people, you'll be cruising.

Now that you have made your choice to break the avoidance cycle and you're ready to stay committed to that, the next most difficult thing you have to learn is how to strike up a conversation. Let's start with the bane of every introvert or socially anxious person: Small talk.

How to make small talk work

There is a way that you can engage in small talk without reducing the conversation to, "Nice weather out!" Unless it's truly a spectacular day or some unusual weather event, talking about the weather is a quick trip to awkward silence as you grapple with what to say next.

Speaking to strangers is uncomfortable for a lot of people. You don't have any common ground to stand on just yet, and you face rejection if the person isn't receptive to talking. On the flip side, being spoken to by a stranger can also feel uncomfortable if you are worried about their intentions or are not prepared to reciprocate. So, I want to leave you with this thought for a moment: Would you consider the world a bright and friendly place? Or is it a gloomy place with conflict and danger at every corner?

Whatever your answer is for that question, you should know that according to an Our World In Data survey, only 35% of people across the globe believe that global living conditions are improving[5] That leaves the majority of people stuck in a pessimistic viewpoint about the world when in fact, many global crises like extreme poverty have been on a steady decline for the last two centuries.

But why am I telling you this? Why does the state of the world have anything to do with small talk?

Well, I'd like you to see small talk as a way to spread positivity between people. Do you think people would have more hope in humanity if what they heard most of the time were positive remarks and compliments? I think so.

There is enough disconnection and negativity in the world, it's time we individually start focusing on spreading a better message about humanity.

Small talk is a great way to interact and connect with the wonderful people who are all around you. It's an incredible way to feel like you belong and to feel confident taking up space in society. If you've ever smiled at a frowning stranger and seen their face light up in return, you'd know that a little bit of love and positivity can go a long way to revealing someone's true nature.

I know that a big reason striking a conversation with a stranger is so daunting is because they aren't giving you any indication that they want to talk. They aren't initiating the small talk, so it's easier to not engage at all. But I want you to consider that many people walk around with a cloud of stressors hanging above their heads.

As you now know, most people are unaware that the world is a better place than it has been in centuries. They may appear grumpy or unapproachable, but upon interaction, you'd be surprised at how quickly you'd see their true colors come through.

What I'm asking you to do here to make small talk easier is give people the benefit of the doubt. Instead of worrying about what they may or may not say to *you*, I want you to approach small talk from a place of brightening someone **else's** day. Some of my favorite techniques for starting a conversation with someone include:

- Offering them a compliment.
- Noticing something you have in common with them.
- Asking them if they're heading to the same event/place as you are.
- Providing assistance to someone who appears lost or upset.
- Expressing interest in something you're both looking at.

Often the reason why it's so difficult to talk to strangers is because you know nothing about them. You have no common ground to start from. You're taking a step into the unknown and that's a scary thing to do. But this chapter is about embracing the unknown.

So, if you can place your focus on how you can serve the other person in some positive way, with a simple compliment, a genuine question, or even a smile, your ability to engage in small talk will transform.

Use your empathy and uncover your curiosity for people. It won't be long until that unknown stranger becomes the neighbor who broke their arm from being kicked by a horse, the bus driver with three kids and a second job, or the old lady who lost her house in the war.

Once you learn something about someone, they are suddenly not so unknown and you see them for what they truly are: Human, just like you.

Please don't take this as me telling you to become a people pleaser. I don't want you to be at the beck and call of every stranger you meet or pass by. What I want you to get from this is a sense of humanity. I want you to realize that people aren't all that bad. You might even learn or experience something great in the most unexpected places.

Small talk is a great practice to become more comfortable around people. The more you feel connected to any old stranger, knowing they are just another person living their lives here on earth, like you, the more you can let go of anxiety in public spaces.

Most people are not out to get you. Your anxiety can make people feel like the enemy. But if you can see that the majority of people are just focused on their own lives and problems, you're going to feel a lot more comfortable around them. Instead of feeling anxious with every unknown person, you will get to know people so well that any stranger can feel familiar.

Small talk can help you gain an understanding of people in general and help you let go of your fear of judgment or perfection around them. If you don't believe me that most people are consumed with their own lives and aren't inherently judging you, you'll soon learn that by engaging with more people.

Holding A Conversation

You can see how starting up a conversation with a stranger, or anyone for that matter, comes down to your willingness to engage with them. But I know that having social anxiety can make you regret opening your mouth at all.

Once you break the ice and start a conversation with someone, holding that conversation without getting overwhelmed or drained can seem impossible. I know the anticipation for how awkward and out of place you feel can put you off engaging with others entirely. But you don't have to be awkward.

Now that you know how to strike up a conversation, and you have a reason to, don't forget about NASA. NASA is your plug-and-play strategy for holding a conversation with confidence. Every social skill you learn will involve NASA in some way. To hold a conversation confidently, you will:

- Non-verbally communicate to show that you are engaged and interested.

- Actively listen to ensure you can keep up and enjoy what is said instead of being stuck in your head.

- Speak effectively to make talking to you easy for the other person.

- Assert yourself to ensure the people you talk to know how to respect you efficiently and help you enjoy the interaction in return.

So if NASA is your basis for communication skills, what's missing? Why do conversations still seem to come to a halt and breed awkward silence, even when you're doing everything right?

Well, something is missing from this equation – what to say. You know *how* to say things correctly, and we've been through some examples of *ways* to say things correctly, but how do you come up with *what* to say?

Awkward Silence Solutions

It's easy to get caught off guard by sudden awkward silence in a conversation. Even though you know how to engage with the other person correctly, if you run out of things to say, an awkward silence can still prevail. But there is a quick solution for awkward silence, it just comes down to your memory.

If you can remember useful conversation starters, you can simply bring one out when the conversation goes dry and see how quickly it flows again. Some of my favorite conversation starters include:

- **Mirroring:** Repeating something someone says in question form. For example: "I went for dinner yesterday and had the most delicious meal." reply with, "Oh, so the meal was delicious?" This should encourage the other person to elaborate.

- **Open-ended questions:** Ask someone something that can't be answered with a simple "yes" or "no." For example: "You're studying science. Why did you go that route?" This will give you a chance to practice listening and inspire more replies. Open-ended questions are "why" questions, but they can also be "how" or "what" questions. For example: "So how did you end up in that situation?" or "What made you want to study that?"

- **Direct requests:** You can continue a conversation by simply asking the other person to keep talking. Use direct requests like "Tell me more?" "I'd love to hear the full story." "Then what happened?" or "Can you explain?"

- **Positive cold reads:** A cold read is an assumption about someone based on characteristics you notice about them. But in this case, you should only make positive cold reads, such as "Nice shoes! You must be a runner?" or "There are rods in your car. Where's your favorite place to go fishing?" Whether your read is accurate or not, you've resurrected the conversation.

- **Ask big questions:** What I mean here is to ask questions that will provoke an excited, long-winded reply such as "What is your biggest goal in life." or "Do you believe in aliens?" Try to keep the questions light-hearted and avoid topics that can cause a heated debate, like politics or religion, unless you know the person really well and know they will enjoy such topics.

Each component of a great conversation works together in unison. It doesn't help knowing all the right things to say without executing them properly or being able to listen in return.

Remember, a massive part of enjoying conversation involves getting out of your head with the strategies you've learned in the first and activating your empathy. That leads us to the next step you have to take to confidently soar through any social setting.

STEP 3: EXPLORE YOUR EMPATHY

I have no doubt that there are people in your life that you care about. I'm sure that when someone truly needs you, you're able to put your anxiety aside and step up to help them – at least, that's what you wish you could do. But even though anxiety can stand in your way of being there for others, having anxiety is a blessing sometimes.

Hear me out.

Anxiety is an awful experience. It activates your fear and can make life miserable. But the beauty of any struggle is that you gain the ability to recognize the struggle in other people and, above all, have empathy for them. It's what you decide to do with that empathy that makes the difference.

That feeling you get when you see someone going through something you may have already been through, the one that makes you remember and internally experience it as a response – that's empathy. Empathy is the art of feeling someone else's perceived emotions in response to their experience.

Let me repeat that: <u>Empathy is your response to the perceived emotions of another person.</u>

It's the same reason why you want to cry when you see someone mourning a loved one. It's why you feel bad when you see someone struggling with homelessness as you drive by in an enclosed car. It's that second-hand embarrassment you get when someone trips and falls in front of everyone. It's your incredible and automatic ability to connect with people.

But, instead of simply feeling empathy for other people, this step is about exploring empathy as a social skill. Empathy isn't only about feeling something from a distance and walking away. You can use empathy to connect with people instantly and have them feel connected to you. But how do you do that?

Think about the first A in NASA. It stands for active listening. Now remember what the most vital component for active listening is – empathy. You can use empathy to help you get out of your head in social situations and bring yourself into the present moment by fully engaging and empathizing with the other person.

The better you are able to show empathy and listen to the person you're talking to, the more you're going to grow a sense of care for them and, ultimately, connection. In return, the more you can make someone feel heard and understood through your ability to empathize, the quicker they will feel comfortable around you and willing to further the connection.

Empathy can serve you in so many ways. With a keen sense of empathy, you will be more likely to enjoy time around people. The same will be true in return. This is because the more empathetic you are with people, the more you will learn about them. And the more you know about people, the easier it is to understand them. This takes us back to overcoming the unknown.

When you understand something better, it becomes known and you are less likely to feel fearful or anxious. Showing empathy for others and learning to understand them is a way of facing the unknown and making it known. When you understand a person better, you can easily anticipate the outcome of spending time with them, giving you confidence around them.

For example, when you take the time to get to know somebody, using your empathy to fully engage with them and make them feel comfortable around you, you will know what to expect from that person. Even if they have bad traits that can get to you, like swearing too much, or talking loudly, if you understand and accept them the way they are, you can enjoy being around them nonetheless. Your empathy allows you to see the truth behind people's negative traits and can help you detach from them instead of taking negative interactions personally.

This is also how you can keep your anxiety in check even when faced with an unpleasant social interaction like conflict or rejection. Your empathy is your ticket to allowing people to be who they want to be without taking their negativity on. You will be able to step back from a bad situation and see the truth behind their behaviors – pain or problems within themselves.

Empathy has many faces. But for the sake of using empathy as a social skill, I want you to try actively exploring your empathy in social situations. Empathy is all about feeling. That means emotions. But it's one thing to automatically feel sad when you see someone crying and another to put thoughts, words, and actions to that sadness.

For this step, I want you to go to your Workbook where you will find an emotions chart waiting for you. It may feel silly, but there are way more emotions than just "happy," "sad," "angry," "excited," etc. And the more you can understand emotions and how to identify them, the less anxious you will feel when encountering someone experiencing a complex emotional situation.

If you can put words to what you're seeing, it'll give you the confidence to handle the situation without losing it yourself. Seeing someone experience a complex emotion, identifying the emotion, and adjusting your response accordingly – that's empathy.

Turn the page in your Workbook and think about an uncomfortable social interaction you've had that seemed to baffle you. Maybe it was conflict with someone close to you, a hostile response from a stranger, or any confusing social interaction you've had.

In your Workbook, I want you to identify what emotions the other person may have been feeling from your empathetic perspective. Put yourself in their shoes and try to imagine how the experience felt for them. Think about the facial expressions they were making. Maybe their tone of voice was different. What kind of body language were they showing?

Write down a description based on the prompts you will find in your Workbook. Now, refer back to your emotions chart and try to choose an emotion that describes how they were behaving.

I've left blank repeats of this exercise for you to use when you have been through an uncomfortable social interaction and are struggling to move past the anxiety it has created. This exercise will help you step into your empathy and improve your ability to understand difficult situations from the other person's perspective.

Another thing you can use to help you overcome confusing social interactions is your conscious thinking. Remember the powerful thinking method you learned in Chapter 3, Book 1? It can help you think and engage more empathetically.

You can use conscious thinking to redirect your thoughts to a more objective place rather than the overwhelming anxious thoughts that may happen during conflict or rejection. For example, instead of:

- "Oh gosh, this person's exploding, I need to run away." try, "Oh gosh, this person is becoming angry. Let me take a deep breath and let them know it's okay."

- "Sarah always snaps at me when I ask about her dad. It hurts me." try, "I can see Sarah is sensitive about the topic of her dad. Maybe she is feeling hurt by him. I should let her know that she doesn't have to talk about him and that I'm here if she wants to."

- "My mom cries about the past all the time. She's such a victim, I don't know what to do." try, "My mom seems sad about the past. Maybe she's still holding onto guilt or pain about what happened. That's perfectly valid and I'll give her time to process it."

- "Jamie gets so frantic when I leave a dirty cup in front of the sink. It's such an overreaction." try, "Jamie has mentioned her OCD in the past. Even though a dirty cup isn't a big deal for me, I can see the disgust on her face. I'll do my best to show her that I understand and will try to be more accommodating."

Can you see how thinking empathetically can lower the stress of a situation? If you practice empathetic thinking patterns, like those in the examples above, you can not only handle difficult situations better, but you may help diffuse them for the other people involved, even if they are the ones causing the problem.

STEP 4: LAUGH A LITTLE

Along with having empathy for others, there's something you should never forget – empathy for yourself. You should care about yourself and how you are enjoying socializing too. But I don't want this to end with empathy, I need you to take it all the way to genuine self-love. Both of these books are about harboring enough self-love that you have the self-confidence and self-esteem to go out and be proud of who you are.

That means you have to learn to let go and detach from what others think of you.

I need you to understand that you are enough. There, I said it. You're enough! The effort you put in throughout these books is to help you realize that. You don't need to become some extroverted "other" version of yourself for people to love your company. No, you're perfectly likable, in fact, lovable, just the way you are.

This also doesn't mean that you don't need to transform. You still have to transform to heal social anxiety and emerge as the social butterfly you are. But you only need to transform into a stronger, healthier version of YOU. If you think you have to become someone you're not to solve your anxiety, then I've failed you. What I need you to do is embrace your value and self-worth so much that you genuinely don't care what people think, say, or do. Easier said than done, right?

Well, there is a way that you can learn to let go and enjoy your life far more. But this method, this "social skill," has layers. It starts with self-love and it ends with the most amazing vulnerability and enjoyment around people. It's all about humor.

Humor, learning to laugh a little, is the next social skill you need to finesse. Sure, being funny can go a long way in making people like you, but that's not what this strategy is about. This strategy is about loving yourself enough to laugh at yourself. Being able to laugh at your own mistakes is humor at its finest.

You need to strike a balance between two things to be able to laugh at yourself when you make a mistake in front of people: Vulnerability and detachment. Let's start with detachment.

The Art Of Letting Go

A major part of having social anxiety is caring too much about what other people think of you. It's often the cause of many catastrophizing thoughts and can make you blow a small mistake way out of proportion. Detachment can help you let go of that. I'll use the example of tripping over in front of a group of people. Just the thought of it can make you uncomfortable.

Let's look at this scenario from the perspective of a socially anxious person, maybe it's you when you started reading this book. Let's call it scenario A: If you were to trip and fall in front of a group of people, you may instantly feel mortified and look up at them expecting the worst. Maybe you worry they're thinking, "Wow, what a clumsy fool. Only a real idiot can fall over like that." Or maybe you expect them to laugh at you. Maybe they do. All around, this scenario has a negative outcome for you. You care

The Butterfly Emerges

deeply about the outcome and whether or not people laugh or think badly of you. You leave unhappy and anxious.

Now let's look at this scenario from the perspective you should have by the end of this book. It's you with all the self-love and confidence you could need. Let's call it scenario B: If you were to trip and fall in front of a group of people, maybe you'd feel a little embarrassed at first and then see the humor in your mistake. Instead of looking to the group to see how they react, you react first by laughing out loud. Even if they start laughing too, you know that it's not because they think you're an idiot, but because it's a silly mistake and they're laughing with you. However, either way, you don't care what they think. In the end, you get up and leave this scenario laughing at yourself and happy. You don't care about the outcome and whether or not people laugh or think badly of you. Your self-worth is high enough not to let others determine your value or reaction.

But how do you get from scenario A to scenario B and become the person who can laugh at themselves so easily? You have to learn to let go and detach from the opinions of others and potential negative outcomes.

You see, the mistake between scenario A and scenario B is exactly the same: you trip and fall in front of a bunch of people. What's different between the good outcome and the bad one is your reaction. Your reaction to any situation makes all the difference. But you can only fix the way you react to things by changing the way you perceive them. Detachment is how you do this.

Detachment is the ability to completely detach from the meaning of a potential outcome. It's when you let go of expectations and simply roll with whatever happens. When you attach too much meaning to a situation, such as worrying about whether people will think you're an idiot if you fall, the outcome starts to matter a lot more to you. Because if you fall, you're an idiot, and you don't want people to think that of you.

If you can let go of your attachment to the situation by saying, "It doesn't matter if I trip and fall. I'm not an idiot either way." Then you won't care what happens. You've already decided beforehand that you're okay with either outcome. Your self-worth is high enough in this scenario not to let the opinions of others affect you.

You can't flip a coin and instantly stop caring what people think. But, as your self-worth and self-confidence grow with the work you continue to do using the methods in the first book, you will be able to detach more easily with time.

Once you have a strong sense of who you are and what matters to you, no one will be able to take that from you. Your identity and value are not determined by who likes you or what people think of you. If you know yourself and love yourself the way you are, silly mistakes are just that – silly. You can learn not to take yourself or other people so seriously and see the humor in silly mistakes.

The truth is that messing up, stumbling, or being awkward sometimes doesn't need to change how people see you. People are far more receptive to your reaction to a "negative" situation than the situation itself. So learn to laugh a little and you'll lighten the mood all around.

With that, there is another important piece to the humor puzzle - vulnerability. Even though humor is found in detachment, its roots are in connection.

The Roots Of Humor
When you laugh at yourself in an embarrassing situation it's known as self-deprecating humor. This kind of humor shows that you can face your limitations and embrace them so no one else can put you down about them. It shows incredible confidence and authenticity.

One of the best ways to succeed and feel confident around people is to be authentic. This means accepting who you are and having no trouble showing your true nature to the people around you. It's also known as being vulnerable.

You'd think that vulnerability makes you weak because sometimes it means exposing your flaws. But vulnerability shows that you are powerfully confident because you aren't afraid to show things that most people won't. Being vulnerable is one of the fastest ways to build human connections.

True connection with people lies in sharing the ugly sides of ourselves. We tend to hide our true selves from most people and only show our best selves out of preservation. But the closer you become with someone, the more your true colors are revealed and your connection either builds or breaks.

To make people feel connected to you instantly, don't be afraid to be vulnerable and expose your true colors early on. One great way to do this is with self-deprecating humor.

I don't mean you should beat yourself up at any chance you get. But you can use your flaws as a humorous talking point in conversation to firstly: make people laugh, and secondly: reveal something about your authentic self.

Remember, your reaction to mistakes teaches people much more about you than the mistake itself. That's why laughing at yourself when you trip and fall can make people like you. It shows that you aren't afraid to be imperfect and that makes people feel connected to you. What did we say about people in Chapter 4, Book1? They aren't perfect and that's a good thing because imperfections bring people together.

So, the easiest ways to make people laugh, and laugh a little yourself, is to let go of attachment and learn to be more vulnerable. The more comfortable you can become with yourself, your flaws, and your self-worth the easier it will be to find humor in an otherwise unpleasant situation.

Again, please don't take this as me saying you have to always be the funny one and try to make people laugh. This strategy is only about lightening up and handling negative situations better so you can attract friends and exude confidence. People pleasing is never okay, and that's where this final strategy comes in.

STEP 5: MANAGE YOUR ENERGY

Social anxiety isn't always turning social invites down, sometimes it's saying yes even when we are exhausted. We say yes hoping to make others happy. But the problem with saying yes when you really want to say no is that you'll be operating at a lower capacity and leaving yourself wide open for anxiety to creep in.

A low social battery means a low energy presence. If you're in company when you really don't want to be, it shows. No matter how good you are at masking your anxiety, people can read each other pretty well. We all have a gut feeling about how the person we're talking to is *really* doing underneath their "I'm fine." That gut feeling is our subconscious picking up on subtle cues like closed-off body language and negative micro-expressions – the tiny facial expressions we subconsciously make that reveal our true feelings.

You're about to dive into the toughest chapter of all and start facing your fears with gradual exposure. That's why this final step is here. You need to know that sometimes pushing yourself to socialize isn't the right thing to do.

Gradual exposure is all about saying "yes" to healthy social situations that would normally scare you. But before you can learn to say "yes," you need to learn to say "no." Managing your social battery is going to help you take charge of your social life and make it work for you.

Everyone has a unique social battery affected differently by different things. Some people get burnt out quickly sitting around a dinner table for hours on end, other people find social media draining. For gradual exposure to work, you need to understand your boundaries and learn how to reserve your energy without becoming a hermit.

Managing In-Person Interaction

To prepare you for Chapter 3, you should know how to reserve your energy even when you're out amongst people. That means monitoring your energy levels and knowing when you've had enough.

You already have a backup plan for if you become overwhelmed – your 5-Step Solution To Solve Fight-or-Flight that you learned in Chapter 5, Book 1. These steps are your plan B. But, for your plan A, I want you to focus on preventative measures. So, here are some of the things you can do to help you recollect yourself and feel re-energized in minutes:

- **Take regular breaks:** Successful socializing isn't always about flat-out one-on-one time with people. There's nothing wrong with needing a short break from the people you're with. If you feel yourself getting a little overwhelmed or anxious, take a quick break to the bathroom or outside, breathe deeply to activate your rest-and-repair response, and recollect yourself before returning.

- **Start small:** Instead of going all-in and approaching strangers on your gradual exposure journey, you can start out by increasing your social expenditure on people you already know and feel comfortable around. This is not the time for "go big or go home."

- **Keep it short:** Monitor your energy levels and if you aren't feeling up to socializing but still want to give it a go, don't be afraid to keep your visit short.

- **Leave when you need to:** Even if you were enjoying your visit at first, if you start to feel drained or overwhelmed and are unable to recharge while out, call it early when you need to. You don't owe anyone your presence. If you are uncomfortable and it becomes too much, leave.

- **Say no:** There are times when even the most social people aren't up for social plans. Just because you're in the process of overcoming social anxiety, doesn't mean you need to ignore your needs and boundaries. If you really want to say no, say no. Just make sure you aren't saying no out of fear when you wish you could say yes.

Prevention is better than cure. Try to monitor your energy levels socially to make sure you don't push yourself too far too fast. I want you to push yourself out of your comfort zone, but I don't want you to do more damage by accidentally creating a new avoidance cycle for yourself. Take this next chapter slowly, and use these tips to help balance comfort with growth.

Managing Social Media

Social media can be a great way to stay connected with people from all over the world. However, don't think that just because it's online it won't affect your social battery. Engaging with people through social media can become a drain on you.

I'm not saying there's anything wrong with having friendships online, but be aware that online friendships still require management to reserve your energy. Most people have some sort of device near them most of the time. Maybe that's your cell phone, tablet, smartwatch, or computer. Unless you start to manage your online social time, you allow people access to you 24/7.

Alone time is important for everyone, even the most confident social butterflies. It gives you a chance to process events and spend time thinking introspectively. But if your phone is constantly buzzing with notifications, you're never truly switching off from socializing. That's a quick way to feel socially drained.

Along with draining your social battery, social media can contribute to social anxiety in other ways. It can encourage you to compare your life to others, make you feel disconnected from the people in your everyday life, and open up opportunities for negative online interactions. It's important that you learn to manage your time on social media and with online friends the same way you do in-person interactions.

However, the most important thing you can do to manage your social media use is to cut off 24/7 access to you. What I mean by this is:

- Turn off notifications from social media apps.

- Delegate time in the day for you to check your apps and engage with people online.

- Block any trolls or online bullies immediately – do NOT engage with them.

- Limit your social media apps to a minimum – for example, choose your two favorites and prioritize your online time for those.

You can consider these practices social media hygiene. If you don't manage your use of the platforms you enjoy, they can become out of hand and start negatively impacting your life. Being bombarded with excessive notifications, dealing with online arguments or mean comments, and having too many social media apps that you check often will drain you.

If you are drained by your time spent on social media you won't have much energy left for in-person connections.

Along with focusing your online time in places that offer authentic connections, like the LearnWell Community, I need you to reserve your energy for positive social interactions. Gradual exposure  requires your full attention, dedication, and perseverance. Managing your energy is an important step to master before deepening your gradual exposure practice.

I don't want you to feel burnt out by anything we do together throughout these books. So as you turn the page to Chapter 3, be prepared to pace yourself and face your fears in a way that is healthy, manageable and, most of all, fun.

FROM FEAR TO FUN WITH GRADUAL EXPOSURE

Steps For Reclaiming Control Over Anxiety Triggers

My body ached from the pressure of lying on a mattress for over 72 hours. 3 days had passed and the only time I had left the bed was to crawl to the bathroom and back. I hadn't eaten, spoken to anyone, nor dared to look outside the door at the scorching daylight. After years of anxiety and depression, a series of traumatic events had triggered an agoraphobic episode.

If social anxiety was on a spectrum between other anxiety disorders, bed-ridden agoraphobia would be on the extreme end. Not only are you too crippled with anxiety to stand and face a crowd, but you're too anxious to stand up at all.

Not eating, moving, or connecting with people for days on end felt a lot like dying. I wasn't sure what was happening to me and I couldn't reach out to the people who cared about me either. I felt alone, sick, and terrified of what was to come if I carried on like that. I knew I wasn't headed anywhere good.

After the fourth day, I was grateful for the pain in my body because it forced me to move. I started sitting up instead of lying down and began processing what was going on. I had never been in this position before. I still couldn't eat or get up for more than a few minutes but this was progress and it gave me the slither of hope I was waiting for. I picked up my phone and called my dad.

Hearing his voice through the phone say "Hello, my sweety" brought me to tears. The familiarity and warmth I felt relieved the intensity of my anxious state for a moment. Sharing that something wasn't right with my dad temporarily lifted anxiety's power over me and allowed me to think. I remembered, just for a minute, who I really am and felt the little spark inside of me again.

That spark, the ounce of fight within you, is the thing that anxiety sets out to dim. It tries to tell you that you're not strong enough to do the things you want to do. If your fight is a flame, fear is water. So, the only way to get yourself up, out of bed, and out the door doing the scary social things you think you can't do is to make your fight bigger than your fear. And that's exactly what I did.

From lying down to sitting up to standing, I took it one tiny step at a time. I figured, "I'm anxious and scared either way, let me just do the scary thing." Each day was like a stop-motion progression of a normal day. Day after day I inched my way to the door. I inched my way to a full bowl of food. And eventually, I inched my way to leaving the house, even just for a moment. Without knowing it, I was making exceptional use of gradual exposure. As the days progressed into weeks, then months, the movie of my life went from stop-motion to film. I could play out a full day's eating, movement, and connection once again.

This is what I need you to do to overcome your social fears. I need you to, inch-by-inch, day-by-day, progress the scene of a healthy and smooth social interaction. I need you to break it down and start small. I need you to acknowledge your fear and do the scary thing anyway. THAT is gradual exposure.

Gradual exposure by definition is the practice of gradually exposing yourself to the activities and things that scare you. It is arguably the best way to build up your confidence and overcome any fear. It is how you can get your spark of a fighting spirit to be bigger and stronger than the waves of fear washing over you. It is how you can break the avoidance cycle of anxiety and set the acceptance cycle into motion.

Now that you have made the decision to take this leap of faith into the unknown and accept the potential positive outcome, it's time to get started. In this chapter, I'm going to walk you through the practical steps you need to take to know where to start and how.

This is where everything you've learned so far is going to converge. Don't lose sight of the effort you've already put into your progress. Wear your progress like armor now as you face your fears and slay them, one by one.

STEP 1: FIND YOUR FEARS

I know you're ready to face your fears because you've made it this far. But until you know what your fears are, clearly and directly, you'll stay stuck in anxiety's grip. Anxiety can feel like a cloud of emotions, thoughts, and sensations that overwhelm you. Finding your fears is all about dissecting your anxiety to pinpoint the exact things that trigger it.

<u>Triggers are any thoughts, situations, or experiences that summon your anxiety to surface.</u>

If you don't know the triggers of your anxiety, you'll only be fighting against the symptoms and not the causes. There's more to social anxiety than just feeling anxious around people. Social anxiety is the combination of experiences, thoughts, and circumstances that create the anxious state. So, to feel confident and enjoy yourself in a social setting, you have to break your anxiety down into its triggers to make healing more manageable.

For example, if social anxiety is a blanket, then I want you to break it down into threads. These threads are your triggers. Focus on unraveling and conquering one thread at a time until you've dissolved the blanket and freed yourself.

You've already been working on your thoughts, so for the sake of gradual exposure, you have to identify the situations and experiences that trigger your anxiety next. Triggers for social anxiety can look like:

- Large crowds
- Dinner parties
- Giving a speech
- Performing live
- Navigating conflict
- Going on a date

Although these are major events and situations that can trigger social anxiety, triggers can also be more simple. Small or simple triggers for social anxiety can look like:

- Greeting a stranger
- Answering a call
- Engaging in small talk
- Being in public alone
- Replying to a text

- Seeing a friend
- Accepting a package
- Asking for help

Go to your Workbook now and follow the prompts to help you put your triggers onto paper. I don't want you to stick to the big triggers for this exercise. Write as many of them down as you can!

You can find out what your triggers are by paying attention to the circumstances, places, people, or events that cause your anxiety to flare up. Think about the last time you went through a social anxiety spell. Who were you with? What were you doing? Where were you going?

As you think, pay attention to your body and how you feel in the present. If you notice your thoughts or emotions becoming anxious as you think about a situation or certain aspects of it, you might be on the trail of a trigger. Look for patterns in your behavior and emotions and try to identify 10 things that trigger your social anxiety. Use the examples above to help guide you.

I want you to take this opportunity to uncover anything that creates a socially anxious reaction in you. Take your time with this exercise, it's going to be important for the next step of gradual exposure.

STEP 2: YOUR FEAR-TO-FUN PYRAMID

With your list of fears, read through the list and take a moment to imagine doing each one. I'm sure some situations seem like a piece of cake to go out and do right away. Yes, they're scary, but you know you could face them if you really had to. However, I know that others on your list feel impossible.

I'm here to tell you that you can overcome every single trigger on that list.

I need you to take your list and organize them into your fear-to-fun pyramid. In your Workbook, you will find an empty pyramid chart with four levels. Write your smaller triggers into the bottom section, your moderately scary triggers into the next section, and your biggest fears into the one above that. And, in the final section, right at the top, write your biggest trigger of all. This is the order in which you are going to prioritize practicing gradual exposure.

The best part about this is that you don't have to worry about facing your biggest fears right away. You have time. Even though gradual exposure is about facing fears and doing scary things regardless of the anxiety they may trigger, with the right pacing, it should be fun. You don't have to dive into the deep end. Gradual exposure is all about dipping in the toe, then the foot, then the leg, until you're ready for full immersion.

Remember, gradual exposure is all about building your confidence, not breaking it. I want you to find a happy medium between your fear and your comfort zone. See each moment you are practicing as a challenge, and don't be afraid to fail or look awkward. Use what you've learned in the previous chapter and practice letting go of perfection.

STEP 3: PREPARE YOURSELF WITH GOALS

With each of your triggers laid out in your fear-to-fun pyramid, I want you to choose the first thing you'd like to overcome. Choose a trigger from the bottom of your pyramid. Make sure it's something challenging and almost exciting. Now, let me show you how to break this trigger down into steps before setting realistic goals for yourself.

Think about what you need to do to overcome this trigger.

Let's use the example of talking on the phone. This trigger is a big deal for some of us. It used to be a huge point of anxiety for me, especially if I didn't recognize the number or was concerned about what the caller wanted. So, a great way to break this trigger down is to think about the process anxiety takes you through when your phone starts ringing.

First: you might hear your ring tone, which may already trigger your fight-or-flight response as the sudden noise jolts you.

Second: you may pick up the phone and try to see who is calling you. If the number is unknown or someone you'd rather not speak to, that could add to the anxiety you feel.

Third: your mind starts battling whether or not you should answer. Anxiety often uses your thoughts to scare you into submission. Maybe you think, "What if they're calling because I'm in trouble" or "What if it's bad news."

Fourth: if you do answer the phone, you may struggle with awkward silences, wonder what to say, or have a hard time listening.

A small, easy task quickly becomes a nightmare with social anxiety. So, to conquer this trigger, you would do three things.

- **One:** Do anything you can to reduce your anxiety in the moment.
- **Two:** Break the task into steps.
- **Three:** Do the scary thing - or at least part of it.

Based on this example, there are some things I would do here:

- **One:** Change my ringtone to something less abrupt. Maybe make it my favorite song or a relaxing melody.
- **Two:** Break the task into steps – taking a deep breath to clear away negative thoughts and prepare to practice NASA for a successful call.
- **Three:** Do the scary thing and answer the call even if I feel anxious.

In your Workbook, you will find a couple of empty pages. Use these pages to break down fears as we proceed. Go there now and break down the first fear you want to overcome. As you work your way up your fear-to-fun pyramid, you might increase the amount of steps it takes to conquer a trigger. The bigger your trigger is, the more steps it might have.

For example, if you want to use gradual exposure to overcome speaking in front of a large crowd, going up on stage and just talking may not be the best approach. For a big trigger like this, it could involve ten or more steps before you can conquer it. A big trigger may even involve overcoming smaller triggers first.

Once you have a basic breakdown of your trigger and feel like you are ready to try gradual exposure, it's time to set goals.

You need to set realistic goals based on where the trigger sits on your fear-to-fun pyramid. If it's at the bottom, don't be afraid to challenge yourself. But if it's at the top, I need you to take it slower. Goals are there to help motivate you. Keep them realistic so you don't end up overwhelmed.

Coming back to the talking on the phone example, you could set goals that look like this:

- **Goal 1:** If my phone rings and it's someone in my contacts list, I must answer it every time for a whole day.

- **Goal 2:** Once I've managed a full day, I must answer every call from my contacts for an entire week.

- **Goal 3:** After a week of successful answers, I must answer any call that I get, regardless of the number, for another week.

- **Goal 4:** Call someone in my contacts list and talk on the phone for at least 10 minutes.

- **Goal 5:** Call a stranger, like the bookings manager at a restaurant, and ask them a question.

Can you see how you can use goals to gradually progress towards fully overcoming a trigger? For this example, you could keep going until you can do all the things that require talking on the phone that you might've struggled to do before.

You can gradually expose yourself to a trigger with as many goals as you'd like. But try to keep it challenging, exciting, and most of all fun! You don't want your goals to spiral you down or drain you. Use them as motivators to conquer your fears one step at a time. Remember what you learned in Chapter 2, you have to manage your exposure to social situations and make sure you respect your social battery. Only do as much as your energy allows in a day.

You can also set up a reward for yourself if you achieve your goal. Celebrating your wins, no matter how small, is what can transform your fear into fun as you look forward to the reward.

A reward can be something related to the trigger, or it can be anything that brings you joy. The most important thing is that the reward matches your achievement. So, if your goal is to answer a call from a friend, make the reward a bar of your favorite chocolate. But if the goal is to face something that is a big deal for you, make the reward something that counts.

I know that social anxiety can make even the smallest social interaction feel like a big deal. And that's where this final stage of gradual exposure comes in – your official step-by-step guide to gradual exposure. This is where you learn the real-life actionable steps you will take each time you go out and face a fear. Call it your field guide if you wish!

STEP 4: YOUR GRADUAL EXPOSURE FIELD GUIDE

This is where I need your full attention. The strategies and methods you've learned up until now have been there to build you up from the inside out. But this is where your journey is about to become very exciting.

You've already transformed your inner world and started embracing the unknown like a caterpillar accepting its fate in order to shapeshift and become something new.

You've built up the knowledge of *how* to overcome your social anxiety, from identifying *why* you feel this way to understanding *what* you need to do.

And, you've made a commitment to yourself that you will conquer your fears and stop avoiding the potential for a positive outcome – no matter what.

Now it's time to let go, embrace the unknown, and DO THE SCARY THING.

To make this process memorable, there are only five parts you need to know. They are the five R's of gradual exposure – Rehearse, Relax, Rethink, Results, Repeat.

To help you remember these steps, look at your hand right now and assign each R to a finger. As you look at each finger, say the R assigned to it. For example, if your thumb is "Rehearse," your index finger is "Relax," your middle finger is "Rethink," your ring finger is "Results," and your pinkie finger is "Repeat."

END YOUR SHYNESS & SOCIAL ANXIETY

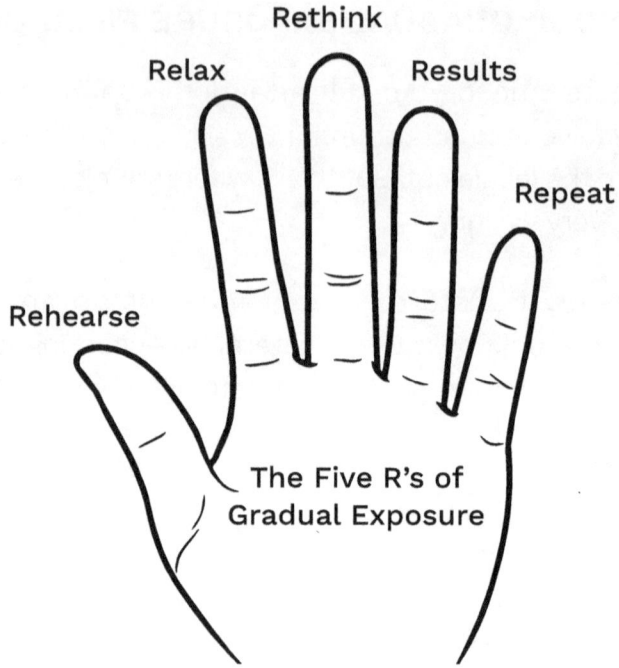

These are the five steps you will use to face any fear from the ground up. Let me break each one down for you before we go into more detail:

- **Rehearse:** Time spent before the exposure activity rehearsing and visualizing a successful outcome.

- **Relax:** Keeping your anxiety under control while you're out doing the scary thing.

- **Rethink:** Paying attention to your thoughts and restructuring them as you go to turn negative thinking into encouragement.

- **Results:** Keeping track of your results, goals achieved, and celebrating your successes!
- **Repeat:** Repeating the steps until you've reached a goal, then use them to work on the next one when you're ready.

These steps take you through the entire process of gradual exposure. You need to have a clear vision of what you'd like to achieve before setting out to do the scary thing. Then, while you do the thing, you need to manage your anxiety levels.

You also need to restructure your thoughts and keep your mind in check so that you build your confidence instead of breaking it. Once it's all said and done, you need to celebrate your progress and reward yourself! I don't want you to lose sight of how far you've come. If you let yourself believe that your successes are a big deal, they will have a big impact on your ability to push yourself further out of your comfort zone.

Lastly, you need to be consistent and dedicated to continuing your healing journey by repeating the practice of gradual exposure. But this is all easier said than done, so let me walk you through each step in this guide.

Rehearse

Your social success starts with your beliefs. If you aren't convinced that you're going to overcome your fears you'll stand in your own way and stop yourself from seeing progress. As you learned in Chapter 1, rehearsing social interactions can help you gain confidence and see yourself as others do. But it can do more than that.

Rehearsing social interactions that scare you can shift your beliefs by making the unknown more known to you. It gives you a chance to "experience" potential outcomes and feel more prepared to handle them.

Just like you can use rehearsing to practice your nonverbal communication skills, you can use your mirror to rehearse entire social interactions. It gives you the chance to see yourself coping with the stress so you can practice better ways to cope before testing it out on other people.

While you can use humor to laugh at yourself if you mess up, I don't want you to use it as a crutch to mask anxiety or pain. This is where rehearsing can save you the trouble. Seeing yourself succeed before you head out into the real-world scenario can shift your beliefs from "can't" to "can."

I want you to practice rehearsing the first trigger you chose to overcome from the bottom of your fear-to-fun pyramid. There is a page in your Workbook waiting for you where you can write down the outcome and prepare for the next try. Open it up, and go to your mirror. Rehearse the scene in the mirror, using your imagination to interact with your hypothetical environment. You don't have to have a back-and-forth conversation with yourself, you can imagine the scenario and respond in real-time.

For example, if you are going to overcome talking on the phone, and your first step is simply answering it, then you can rehearse how you will answer. Practice different ways until you find one that you are proud of. Maybe you go from a measly "Hello?" to a confident "Hi! How are you?" Use this time to really get comfortable with the situation you are going to face in person soon.

Once you're done rehearsing the scene, go back to your Workbook and fill out the questionnaire to help uncover your strengths and weak points. Use this information to refer back to after you've given the real-world scenario a try and improve for the next time.

There is another way that I'd like you to rehearse facing your trigger before moving on. I want you to use the visualization technique you learned in Chapter 5, Book 1 – Positive Social Revisualization. This is when you sit in meditation and visualize the scenario in your mind. But I don't want you to visualize it mindlessly, I want you to use this practice to show yourself what potential positive outcomes are possible for your scenario.

Remember, prevention is better than cure. That is why this first step is so lengthy. How you prepare yourself before doing the scary thing is going to make a tremendous difference to the outcome. I need you to prevent breaking your confidence as much as possible. That's where visualization works its charm. You'll find these instructions in your Workbook too:

- **Step 1:** Find a quiet place to sit or lie down comfortably undisturbed for a few minutes.

- **Step 2:** Bring your awareness to your breathing and focus on taking nice deep breaths for a few moments until you can feel yourself relaxing and fully engaged in the exercise.

- **Step 3:** Visualize facing the anxiety trigger and simply let your mind reveal the outcome. Don't judge what you see. Just allow it to unfold, even if it is negative.

- **Step 4:** Whatever the outcome of the situation is, let it go. You have to release your expectations for the outcome to make space in your mind for a better one. You can also use this opportunity to giggle and appreciate how creative your mind can be! Don't take this process too seriously. Allow your mind to flow with the images.

- **Step 5:** Once you have released the initial expected outcome you played out in your mind's eye, focus on your breathing again to clear your mind.

- **Step 6:** Now, intentionally visualize the same scenario, but this time, try to imagine the best possible outcome. Let the scene play out slowly, and take in the emotions you feel seeing your success unfold in front of you.

- **Step 7:** When you're ready, open your eyes while holding this intention for a successful outcome.

You can see rehearsing in the mirror as your practical practice to prepare yourself and visualizing as a way to mentally prepare yourself. Visualizing forms part of a mindfulness practice which is a powerful tool to conquer your thoughts and fears.

Take a moment to do both of these rehearsal methods before you face the fear in the real world. Then, once you feel prepared and armed with a positive intention for the outcome, move on to the second R - Relax.

Relax

I need you to know that no matter how prepared you feel to face your fear, your fight-or-flight response is likely still going to kick into gear. Maybe you won't have a panic attack, but your anxiety is still going to play up. That's why focusing on your relaxation skills is the next fundamental thing you must focus on during gradual exposure.

If you think that you should be able to do all the things on your pyramid with ease, I'm going to let you in on a secret: even some of the most experienced actors, performers, or live presenters still get anxious before they do their thing. That's because many of the things that are high up on your fear-to-fun pyramid are scary things for anyone to do.

Even though social anxiety makes things that most people find easy very difficult, the principle is the same. You might get more comfortable doing the things that scare you, but to some degree, they might still trigger anxiety. The key here is knowing how to soothe it and move on quickly.

You learned how to help prevent overwhelm in the previous chapter by pacing yourself to manage your energy. Those tips are still extremely relevant here. Use them. But sometimes intense anxiety isn't preventable and you need a solution. Now that you're prepared and have rehearsed overcoming the fear that you've selected, I'm going to take a moment to remind you of your 5-Step Solution To Solve Fight Or Flight from Chapter 5, Book 1:

- **Step 1:** Deep breathing
- **Step 2:** Mindfulness meditation
- **Step 3:** Visualization
- **Step 4:** Progressive muscle relaxation
- **Step 5:** Self-care practices

You've already used step 3 to help you prepare yourself and calm your anxiety beforehand, but it can still form part of your relaxation efforts. It's time to use all five steps to manage your anxiety levels while you're in the real-world experience. Here is how I want you to use them:

- **Deep breathing:** When you feel your heart race or your thoughts become erratic, take a couple of deep breaths and allow them to release the tension in your body and clear your mind. You can take a deep breath at any point during a social interaction, or you can take a moment to leave the situation and calm yourself using your breath.

- **Mindfulness meditation:** If you feel yourself becoming overwhelmed in the slightest, remember that anxiety detaches you from the present moment. Use the grounding technique you learned in Chapter 5, Book 1, and ground your senses back into the present to regain your power.

- **Visualization:** This is a great opportunity for you to use the anxiety relief visualization from Chapter 5, Book 1. Take a moment to close your eyes and visualize yourself in a place you feel safe and calm. Over time this can become like a reflex and will trigger relaxation just by thinking of the place for a few minutes.

- **Progressive muscle relaxation:** You can't always find a place to sit or lie down privately to practice PMR. But you can use PMR secretly during a social interaction that you find challenging. For example, if you're sitting at a dinner table, you can clench and release your fists out of sight to help release some of the tense energy in your body.

However, you can take a moment to go to a restroom or your car and work on contracting and releasing your more obvious muscles.

- **Self-care practices:** Although self-care is more often a practice to help keep your anxiety levels down in everyday life, there are ways you can implement self-care to relieve anxiety while you're facing a fear. For example, you can use essential oils like lavender and apply some to your wrists or clothing to help you stay calm and grounded. You can bring a fun fidget toy like a stress ball or a fidget cube to help you meet your need to fidget in social settings if you struggle with that. You can wear noise-reduction earplugs if you struggle with the noise of a large crowd. Self-care is all about respecting and meeting your needs. Don't be afraid to do so in a social setting if it will help calm you without bothering anyone else.

With all these tools and techniques at your disposal, you can feel confident that you are equipped to manage your anxiety. Make use of everything you've learned and apply them to your present situation while you conquer any given trigger.

Anxiety is a natural human response to stressful situations. Don't let it discourage you from your efforts to overcome fears. Expect it and learn to manage it in the moment.

To keep your anxiety at a minimum and guarantee your success, don't get ahead of yourself. Remember that you're not here to rip the bandaid off. You're here to gradually expose yourself to your triggers so that you can expect only as much anxiety as you can manage at a time.

If you start to feel overwhelmed, you're going too fast. Slow down and know that it's okay to take your time or go back to basics. So many things can influence your anxiety levels. Stay receptive to your anxiety and adjust your pressure and goals accordingly. It doesn't matter how slow you go, any progress is still a success.

Rethink

By now, I know that you've done a lot of work on your thinking patterns and false beliefs. Transforming your thoughts was one of the first things you had to conquer on this journey.

In Chapter 3, Book 1, you learned to identify negative thinking patterns to restructure your thoughts and think in a more consciously productive way. Gradual exposure will challenge your progress as you step out of your comfort zone and face your triggers.

Your false beliefs are the number one reason why you have triggers in the first place. Part of overcoming them means facing the thoughts that accompany them and identifying the beliefs behind them. While you're out conquering your fears, I need you to pay close attention to your thinking patterns. Try to see if they are helping you succeed or bringing you down.

If you can identify any of the three cognitive distortions that anxiety can cause, that is a bonus! Just to remind you, they include:

- Catastrophizing
- Black and white thinking

- Overgeneralization

Most negative thoughts caused by anxiety fall under one of these categories. But I want you to pay attention to your inner voice as well. Listen to how you speak to yourself in these potentially stressful moments. If you find yourself beating your efforts down or getting stuck in cognitive distortions this is when you need to step up and take back your control.

You're going to use conscious thinking, also known as cognitive restructuring, to help you reclaim your thoughts and transform them from enemies to allies in real time.

You already know how to do this, but here is a recap of your Conscious Thinking Action Plan from Chapter 3, Book 1:

- **Step 1:** Challenge negative thoughts
- **Step 2:** Reframe negative thoughts
- **Step 3:** Practice positive self-talk
- **Step 4:** Slowly shift false beliefs
- **Step 5:** Try cognitive behavioral therapy

The first three steps to this plan are the most important for gradual exposure. These are the steps that you can implement in real life situations to help you take better care of your thoughts. The more you do this, the more your beliefs will slowly shift automatically. You can also use what you learn from cognitive behavioral therapy to help you with gradual exposure.

Facing a trigger is never easy, even if you see it as a fun challenge. I want you to pay special attention to Step 3 and make an effort with your positive self-talk. Your words are a powerful tool to help invoke a sense of courage within yourself. They can help you feel determined to carry on trying no matter how anxious you feel.

This is a great time to make use of mantras. There has never been a better time to remind yourself, "I am safe" than right now. Mantras can help you remember that you're okay in the midst of a challenging social situation or setting.

Words can influence your thoughts which have an effect on your emotions and behavior. Use mantras like "I am safe" to help you feel relaxed and ready to face the challenge. Other mantras you could use include:

- I can handle this.

- Anxiety does not control me.

- I am me and that's all I have to be.

- I am safe in this space.

- I've got this.

- It's just anxiety. It won't kill me.

You will find a list of useful mantras in your Workbook. Choose the ones that resonate with you the most and feel exciting to say. The more emotions a mantra sparks within you, the better it will work. There is also a blank list for you to fill with your own mantras over time. Write your favorite mantras down there or make up your own. Have fun and see if you can make one or two rhyme!

I need you to stay on top of your thoughts and inner voice to help you feel encouraged and motivated to continue with your gradual exposure practice. The more you build a sense of safety within yourself, the more you will carry that safety net wherever you go.

Results

No matter the outcome of your gradual exposure attempts, I want you to make a record of the highs and lows of the experience. Even a failure can be a success if you learn from it. Go to your Workbook now and see the pages waiting for you. You can use these pages to document your experience facing a trigger. Journaling is a great way to keep track of your progress and see how far you've come. When you run out of pages, simply use the same questions in a new journal.

For each trigger you address on your fear-to-fun pyramid, I want you to start a new progress sheet. Write down the highs and lows of each attempt until you feel confident that the trigger is resolved.

A resolved trigger does not always mean no anxiety whatsoever. I want you to view your success as an improvement in how you cope with the trigger. Many bigger triggers are always going to involve some form of anxiety, but when you have the confidence to handle it smoothly, without letting the anxiety overwhelm you, you can consider it a success.

The next, and most important thing I need you to do when it comes to your results is celebrate your successes. Even the smallest wins deserve your acknowledgment and celebration. After all, gradual exposure is all about collecting little wins that lead up to big wins.

This is your time to reward yourself for achieving goals and giving yourself the praise you deserve. Even if it's simply saying well done or feeling a sense of accomplishment after you do something that scares you – Don't let your efforts go unnoticed.

Repeat

Once you've made an attempt to overcome a trigger and have celebrated your small success, repeat the process until the trigger is resolved. When you have achieved a goal or resolved a trigger, choose a new goal or trigger and repeat the process until they are resolved too. Work your way up your fear-to-fun pyramid and do your best to enjoy as much of the process as you can.

Keep finding ways to see the humor in your failures, and don't let them stop you from trying. Gradual exposure is about overcoming your fears step-by-step so don't worry if it takes you a while to do all the things you want to do. Be patient with yourself and trust the process.

I don't want you to feel unprepared in any way. Before we move on to Chapter 4, there is a hidden "R" that you need to know about in this field guide. This "R" is for when things go horribly wrong and you don't know where to turn. It stands for Retrace. I don't want it to be a part of your five "R" field guide because I want you to prepare for the best. But if you feel stuck at any point along your gradual exposure journey, simply retrace your steps and go back to the previous ones if you need to.

Sometimes this means spending more time rehearsing your trigger, relaxing your mind and body for longer, or taking time out to pause and work on your thoughts until you are able to continue exposing yourself to the trigger again. There is no shame in needing to take a break or go back to basics. Only do what is helping your growth, not what may hinder it.

While you put this field guide to practice and work on the triggers in the bottom layer of your pyramid, Chapter 4 is going to help prepare you for some of the triggers that may be higher up.

You can conquer many social hurdles on your own with gradual exposure, but others need a little bit more backstory to help you soar over them. Turn the page now and be ready to learn what it will take to overcome a few of the biggest social hurdles, from job interviews and public speaking to romantic dates and conflict.

SKIP OVER THE USUAL SOCIAL HURDLES

How Self-Compassion And Understanding Create Social Comfort

Quick! Say something nice about yourself. Name one thing you really like about who you are. Do it now, I'll wait! I want you to begin this chapter with a real sense of appreciation for yourself. You've come a very long way and you deserve to give yourself a little credit...scratch that, a LOT of credit.

I know you've been working hard to heal your social anxiety. The kind of progress you've already seen doesn't happen overnight. It takes dedication, effort, and tremendous courage. Don't let that go unnoticed. I need you to see your progress for what it is – nothing short of amazing!

Once you realize how much of a fighting spirit you have and can now see how far it's taken you, I don't want you to even bat an eye at what comes next. You're ready to tackle the things that are higher on your fear-to-fun pyramid. Don't worry, you won't be doing it alone, I'm here to help guide you all the way to the top.

In this chapter, I'm going to walk you through tips and strategies for overcoming some common but big social anxiety triggers. Whether they are on your fear-to-fun pyramid or not, you need to pay attention. The strategies for successfully facing these major fears are applicable to many of the big fears you have written in your pyramid.

Before we continue, there is one consistent theme you'll notice throughout every strategy here – self-compassion. Just like you gave yourself a compliment at the start of this chapter, I want you to keep that energy alive as we continue.

Tackling your biggest fears is going to involve some failure. I need you to be strong enough to love yourself through it all.

Failures without self-compassion often lead to self-criticism and punishment. There is no value in that. Encouragement to get up and keep trying is the way.

I need you to use your inner voice to help motivate you. Speak to yourself with kindness and remember to celebrate every small win you make. Let's keep it simple, hold the gradual exposure field guide in mind, and get started.

The big social anxiety triggers I'm going to reference include:

- Conflict
- Public speaking
- Rejection
- Dating
- Job interviews
- Criticism

I know you might have different fears than these, like performing in front of people or making new friends. However, I also know you will still find the value you're looking for to overcome your fears using the strategies throughout this chapter.

You see, certain fears can be grouped into categories based on various harmful patterns. Whether your biggest anxiety trigger is listed here or not, it will likely be a result of one of three root patterns – Self-neglect, self-doubt, or self-deprecation.

These root patterns feed off of each other, so there is plenty of overlap between the strategies you use to overcome each of them. Self-neglect is often the root pattern behind difficulty handling conflict and criticism. Self-doubt is often the root pattern behind problems keeping up new connections and dealing with rejection. Self-depreciation can cause the approval of others to outweigh your own, creating anxiety from public speeches and interviews. It is not to be confused with self-deprecating humor, and I'll tell you why shortly.

I want to take a moment here to remind you again that nobody is perfect. Everyone struggles with one of these three root patterns from time to time. But when these problems overtake the truth for you and cause deep-rooted false beliefs, social anxiety, or other forms of anxiety, often manifests.

Naturally, struggling with any of these root patterns can affect your ability to cope all around. But because the goal of this chapter is to help you tackle your biggest anxiety triggers, I'm diving straight to their roots to solve the problems where they start.

Moving forward, I still need you to use gradual exposure to overcome whatever fear you're working on. But alongside your daily efforts to reach your fear-to-fun goals, I want you to work on undoing the root pattern behind the fear.

For each of the three root patterns, I'm going to give you strategies to help break them. Once you start dissolving the patterns behind your biggest fears, you'll start seeing them for what they really are – an illusion. They are not based on reality, only the perceptions we adopted from negative experiences, other people, trauma, and other external influences.

Your biggest social fears are based on false perceptions caused by negative experiences, other people's influence, trauma, and more.

Let me repeat that: Your biggest social fears are based on false perceptions caused by negative experiences, other people's influence, trauma, and more.

In a nutshell, overcoming your biggest fears involves correcting your false perceptions with compassion and self-love. So, if you're ready to learn how to use these two powerful positive tools to make it to the top of your fear-to-fun pyramid, let's dive in!

SELF-NEGLECT

At the root of problems handling conflict or criticism is often some form of self-neglect. Maybe you don't have the communication skills to cope with conflict, or you may have a history of critical parents that makes criticism feel traumatic. Regardless of the reasoning behind your experience, self-neglect is the root pattern that reinforces these problems.

Self-neglect is a pattern that is often created by experiences and interactions that made you question your worth. If you subconsciously fed into this question of your worth and formed a false belief that you aren't good enough then you may have acquired a tendency to undervalue yourself. You might neglect yourself by criticizing yourself, or not standing up for yourself during conflict.

If you don't see your value, you will likely neglect your need for self-compassion. You may bring yourself down with negative thinking and harmful beliefs about yourself. A pattern of self-neglect can also cause you to see criticism as an attack and make you feel like the victim. Neither of these perspectives does anything good for you.

Now for the solution to self-neglect – self-love! You have to create a new pattern for yourself that becomes so ingrained in you that it erases the old one. Instead of practicing self-neglect, I need you to start focusing on self-love.

Instead of breaking yourself down, I need you to build yourself up. You need to reveal your true worth to yourself so you can see and accept how valuable you are. Once you know that you deserve to be treated right by others and that you matter, you won't feel so powerless during conflict or so hurt by criticism. Some self-love techniques you can try to built your self-worth include:

- Mindfulness
- Positive affirmations
- Self-care

You already have a good idea about how to practice mindfulness, you learned the basics of mindfulness in Chapter 5, Book 1. You also learned how to implement self-care into your healing journey. To add to these practices and heal self-neglect by building your self-worth, I want to teach you about positive affirmations.

Words have power.

Hacking Your Subconscious Mind With Positive Affirmations

I'll say it again just for good measure: Words have power.

Positive affirmations will remind you of the mantras you've been using throughout these books. Some of them *are* positive affirmations. But mantras are more about making you feel a certain way, whereas positive affirmations are there to help you be a certain way.

Positive affirmations are "I am" statements. There are no spoken words more powerful for your self-worth than these. Why? Because you are literally speaking who you truly are in the present moment. You're pulling your best self out from beneath the fear that has brought you down.

Think about it. Positive affirmations aren't "I will be" statements. They're not "I want to be" statements. They are "I am" statements. Here are some examples I want you to try:

- I am lovable.
- I am kind.
- I am capable.
- I am worthy.
- I am resilient.

A great positive affirmation takes you all the way to the end result. You won't say "I am healing," you would say "I am healed." And there is a reason for that.

Studies show that practicing positive affirmations activates the reward system in your brain. However, when used regularly, the practice builds into something more – an improved sense of self-confidence. Researches also noted a resilience to resistance against your self-worth.[6]

That means that positive affirmations can help you see your self-worth and capabilities in such a profound way that you won't tolerate others trying to put you down – let alone yourself.

You can use positive affirmations the same way you would mantras, by repeating them to yourself in a difficult situation, such as "I am calm" or "I am kind" during an argument. However, I don't want you to stop there. Affirmations work best when you repeat them regularly throughout the day. And they work even better first thing in the morning and just before bed.

Affirmations work with your subconscious mind to build up positive beliefs about yourself. To save you the technical jargon of brain waves, all you need to know is that when you wake up and when you fall asleep, your subconscious mind is the most absorbent. This is because your subconscious is most active while you sleep.

It's the same reason why the TV adverts that tend to get stuck in your head the most happen late at night when you're practically half asleep on the sofa. Some advertisers know that your brain is more likely to subliminally take in the message of the advert late at night and potentially cause you to choose one product over another.[7]

Just like advertisers try to hack your brain waves to remember products, I want you to hack your brain waves with positive affirmations. There are various ways that you can try to inject "I am" statements into the hours where you are the most susceptible to taking in your desired message. Some ways that I recommend include:

- Sticking "I am" statements on your bathroom mirror.
- Making your phone wallpaper an image with an "I am" statement.
- Listening to relaxing music before bed overlayed with "I am" statements.
- Repeating "I am" statements in your mind as you fall asleep.
- Practicing a morning meditation with "I am" statements.

There are other times in the day when positive affirmations are more readily absorbed as well. Just like when you are in a waking or sleep state, your mind is also more absorbent to affirmations when you're on autopilot.

For example, when you're driving the same route to work every morning or taking a run on the same trail, your subconscious mind may become more active. As you enter that autopilot state that can make you lose track of time or get to where you're going without consciously being aware of what you're doing, affirmations will get another chance to enter your subconscious.

Remember, the subconscious mind is where your false beliefs are formed. To undo false beliefs and stop negative patterns like self-neglect, you have to get your self-worth to translate in your subconscious mind as well.

This takes repetition, so don't be disheartened if it takes some time to start working. Practice discipline and stick to the things you've learned here for some time before giving up hope. Once your root pattern starts to resolve as your self-worth grows and your false beliefs shift, you will feel the change.

While you patiently trust the process of self-love, don't forget about the practical strategies you have learned throughout these books. NASA can help you deal with negative interactions with others just as well as it works for positive ones. Remember to be assertive of your needs and boundaries, and tap into your empathy to allow you to cope with other people's emotions. You can refer back to your emotions chart to help you out.

SELF-DOUBT

The second root pattern responsible for many big social fears is self-doubt. When you doubt yourself, it shows that you lack confidence. Along with causing social anxiety at the best of times, a lack of confidence can make you anticipate rejection as you doubt your ability to win over friends and form romantic connections.

Doubt can make you hesitate in your natural social instincts causing you to come across as awkward or distant. Positive dating experiences thrive on relaxation, comfort in another person's presence, and genuine connection.

If you're doubting yourself and fearful of rejection, dating can become a scary experience rather than an exciting one. When you're stuck in an anxious state, you won't be able to make your date feel comfortable around you or show your best self off. The same goes for new friendships.

<u>When you expect rejection, you kill the connection.</u>

Unfortunately, I can't appease you by saying you can avoid rejection. Sometimes you can't. Rejection is a natural part of life and it happens all the time to everybody. Instead of letting rejection scare you, I want you to work on accepting it.

However, don't confuse accepting rejection with expecting it. Expecting it means you waste time anticipating rejection. The expectation of rejection causes anxiety and stops you from showing up as your true self. But when you can accept rejection by learning to cope with it, you can overcome your fear of it and enjoy new social environments.

Self-doubt makes accepting rejection very difficult. It is, more often than not, the root pattern behind a fear of rejection. In the same breath, a fear of rejection is more often than not the cause of dating anxiety.

There are more reasons why you may fear dating or romantic connections – I'm not going to talk about the fear that stems from trauma here, but purely fear that stems from social anxiety. Social anxiety that causes a fear of dating can often be traced back to a root pattern of self-doubt. You may fear that you will mess up, make a fool of yourself, or face rejection.

When you expect rejection, you kill the connection.

While you work on healing your social anxiety as a whole, you can take steps to let go of a fear of rejection and dating by releasing self-doubt and embracing self-confidence. You already know how to build your self-confidence from Chapter 4, Book 1, so go back and keep practicing what you've learned to help you here. Just to remind you, you need to:

- Prioritize progress over perfection
- Practice self-care to build your self-confidence
- Show up for yourself as your primary support system
- Practice gratitude to shift your mindset

Worrying about rejection can stand in your way of connecting with potential new friends or romantic partners. If a pattern of self-doubt is the likely culprit behind one of your biggest fears, focus your efforts on building your self-confidence and easing into new connections with the social skills you learned in Chapter 2.

Replace rejection with authentic connections and watch your self-doubt disappear. Remember that it's okay to be a little awkward sometimes. Laugh it off and don't worry about being perfect. Authenticity is more likely to win over your new friend or date than getting worked up about any potential mess-ups. Go easy on yourself, and show yourself a little compassion.

SELF-DEPRECATION

It may seem contradictory because of what you learned in the "Laugh a little" section of Chapter 2, but self-deprecation can be extremely harmful. As you know, self-depreciation is when you point out your flaws. However, the difference between self-deprecating humor and a pattern of self-depreciation is your intentions and the effect it has on you.

Instead of showing how comfortable and confident you are with your flaws, the self-depreciation root pattern is a form of self-loathing. It is when you fixate on your flaws and constantly put yourself down about them. It can include beating yourself up for small mistakes and having a negative internal voice that says things like, "Why am I like this?" "I can never do anything right." "Nobody likes me." or, I'm such an awkward loser." and breaking your self-esteem down.

Although the overlap here is that a fear of public speaking and job interviews can be gravely affected by self-doubt and self-neglect, self-depreciation is the biggest culprit. You can certainly use the strategies from the rest of this chapter to help you face these two big fears, but above all, I need you to focus on breaking your self-depreciation pattern.

Self-deprecation can show up and ruin your attempts to overcome a fear of public speaking or job interviews as you think thoughts such as "I probably won't get the job anyway," or "I'll try my best but we all know how clumsy and awkward I can be." Sometimes self-depreciation doesn't show up in the form of thoughts at all. It can show up in how you feel.

You may not even realize that you self-deprecate until you start to question your fear and look a little deeper. It can reveal itself in your false beliefs and a sense of apathy. It can also cause you to rely on the validation and approval of others since you can't rely on yourself for those.

It won't matter how many public speaking or job interview tips you learn. If your deepest root pattern keeps you small, your fear will persist. Even if the tips are expert-level, much of your effort and learning will be in vain. That's why addressing the root patterns behind any fear is so important.

To break the pattern of self-depreciation, you need to build your self-confidence and harbor an unbreakable trust within yourself. You need to trust your own validation and approval above anyone else's. This way, you can face rejection at a job interview or a bad audience during public speaking and walk away with your self-esteem intact.

Once again, you learned how to build your self-confidence in Chapter 4, Book 1. Apply what you learned there to your journey of overcoming a fear of public speaking, job interviews, or any other fear rooted in self-deprecation. However, most importantly, make sure you focus on improving your inner voice. Use your voice to form a pattern of self-appreciation and encouragement instead.

Remember what you learned in Chapter 3, Book 1, you need to speak to yourself like a friend. The same goes for encouragement. Cheer yourself on in your head when you face situations you're scared of the way you would cheer on a friend doing something they're scared of. Use mantras like, "I've got this!" to help you out. You can speak to yourself using "you" instead of "I." For example, tell yourself, "You've got this!" in your head to really help the encouragement translate.

Your inner environment will determine how relaxed and confident you are when facing big fears. Make it a nurturing and compassionate place, and you won't be so easily broken down by stress or failures. No one can stand up on the stage and encourage you while you're actively doing the scary thing, so make a habit of encouraging yourself.

You should know that the social hurdles at the top of your fear-to-fun pyramid will not dissolve overnight. Breaking negative patterns and forming positive ones is a long-term solution. As you learned in Chapter 3, Book 1, social anxiety doesn't form overnight either, which is why long-term solutions work the best.

Since Chapter 1, Book 1, you've been walking the long-term healing path for your social anxiety. You are fully equipped to soar over any social hurdle, no matter where it is on your fear-to-fun pyramid. You're also ready to focus on the joy and fulfillment positive social connections can bring. But there is one last thing I need you to do to make sure your social success lasts forever – stay social! In this next and final chapter, I'm going to show you how.

5

STAYING ON TRACK & STAYING SOCIAL

How To Integrate This New Freedom Into Your Life, Forever

You've come a long way since you opened this book. Your progress is incredible and you deserve to be as proud of yourself as I am of you right now. You're no longer that shy reader who started these books in hopes of finding answers – you've found your answers and you're not looking back.

While this is the final chapter of the books, it is an early part of your healing journey. The progress you've seen is only the start of what's to come. However, if you close this book and leave everything you've learned here on these pages, you risk letting fear drown out your inner flame again.

As we have reiterated throughout, every strategy of your healing journey has a role to play – each one is a cog in your social recovery system. To continue seeing progress, you have to keep everything in alignment. The same goes in reverse. If one cog of social anxiety starts to turn slowly, the others will follow until you're stuck in an avoidance cycle once again.

Now that you've made significant progress, I need you to keep the wheels of recovery turning. I want you to keep striving for more social fun and fulfill your dream of long-term unbreakable confidence. I want you to let your social butterfly wings glisten in the sun as you laugh, tell stories, and grow meaningful connections with others.

This chapter holds the final thing I need you to dedicate yourself to if you want to leave social anxiety in the past for good. I need you to stay social. Don't worry, it's not all on you. I'm about to give you the guidelines on how to stay on track and keep healing forever. Those conga lines and dinner parties are yours for the taking!

RECOVERY IS A JOURNEY, NOT A DESTINATION.

You should know that healing has no ending. There are always more ways for you to grow. That doesn't mean your pursuit is pointless, only that there is no finish line. The beauty in having no finish line is that it's not a race. As long as you're making progress, you are winning.

Recovery is a journey, not a destination. There is no perfect end result. As cliche as it sounds, life really is full of ups and downs. No matter how much you've healed, life's challenges will always be there to test you.

One of the biggest mistakes I've made on my healing journey is to get lazy with my self-care and relaxation techniques. When things are good, it's easy to forget about why you're coping so well. Sometimes your relaxation and self-care practices are so effective that you feel on top of the world and start letting them slip. This leaves gaps for anxiety to sneak its way back in.

The trouble with anxiety is that once it's taken hold of you, remembering the techniques that worked for you before can feel flighty. It can make you forget how far you've come and trick you into thinking you never healed at all. That's not true.

Remember, recovery is a journey. There is no perfect reality you can work towards where anxiety doesn't exist at all. Anxiety is a natural part of life. It's your ability to cope with it and nip it in the bud before it overtakes you that counts.

A quick reminder: prevention is better than cure.

Learn from my mistake. I want you to focus on maintaining the relaxation techniques you've learned to reduce the risk of social anxiety trying to reclaim its throne over you. That means making it a part of your daily routine whether you're anxious or not.

Here is a quick recap of all the things you can use to stay socially stable and relaxed:

- Deep breathing
- Mindfulness meditation
- Visualization
- Progressive Muscle Relaxation
- Self-care practices
- Energy Management

Keeping up your relaxation practice will not only help you maintain manageable levels of anxiety, but it will help you cope in every aspect of your life. If life's ups and downs are waves, think of your self-care and relaxation techniques as the surfboard allowing you to ride them. Cowabunga!

YOUR MIND IS YOUR GREATEST ALLY

Like a parasite, anxiety is always looking for ways to creep up on you and lay down its roots – your thoughts are no exception. I'd go as far as to say that they are the first place social anxiety shows up. Sure, your body may show signs of anxiety as you anticipate a social event, but once you start feeling anxious, it's likely that your thoughts have already been working against you.

Sometimes even the best relaxation techniques won't calm your mind. That is why you must keep your mind in check as much as possible. If you let your mind run wild without reinforcing your positive inner environment, you risk negative thinking becoming a pattern again. That can include the three cognitive distortions of catastrophizing, black-and-white thinking, or overgeneralization.

Your thoughts can either be your greatest ally or your greatest enemy. It's up to you to choose. Whether things are going well or bad, I need you to continue working on your thoughts. Remember, negative thinking patterns are often a result of false beliefs. These can take a very long time to shift. Even after you close this book, you need to continue working on keeping your thoughts constructive.

Thoughts have a way of either building you up or spiraling you down. One negative thought can breed into another until you're riddled with low self-esteem or other false beliefs about yourself. But, positive thoughts can be contagious too. Let's recap on the positive thinking techniques I need you to continue making use of:

- Challenge negative thoughts
- Reframe negative thoughts
- Practice positive self-talk
- Slowly shift false beliefs
- Cognitive behavioral therapy
- Repeat helpful mantras
- Practice positive affirmations

With time and practice your brain will become so accustomed to thinking constructively that it won't be such an effort anymore. You will naturally become a more conscious thinker rather than someone who allows their automatic thoughts to hold any weight. Remember, they're just thoughts! Your reaction to your thoughts and the actions you choose to take based on them is far more important.

Just like you need to keep up your immune function to reduce your chances of falling ill, you need to nurture and maintain a healthy inner environment to keep the parasite of anxiety from taking control of your thoughts, emotions, and actions. A healthy inner environment equals a healthy and happy you.

COMFORT KILLS GROWTH

Now that you know that recovery is a journey, I don't want you to become complacent. To see the lasting change you want to see, you have to stay committed to your growth. That means daily effort to stay above challenges, as well as continuing to pursue your fear-to-fun goals.

I need you to see gradual exposure as a part of your lifestyle. No, you don't have to go out and make small talk with strangers or stand up and do a speech every day, but you have to balance comfort and growth.

If you're too comfortable with the progress you've made, you will stunt your potential for further improvement. Even if you've already mastered the fears at the bottom of your pyramid, don't stop yourself from moving forward out of fear. I want you to carry on with your gradual exposure practice forever.

Even when you've faced the fear at the very top of your fear-to-fun pyramid, I want you to see gradual exposure as a lifestyle choice to constantly improve yourself and overcome any fear in life. Don't limit this incredible practice to overcoming social anxiety. You can use it for so much more.

Maybe you struggle with depression, chronic stress, or habits that don't serve you. Use what you've learned about gradual exposure to help you become more brave and more resilient to setbacks in general. It is the perfect practice to develop a growth mindset, something that can help you become successful in every way.

Remember, a growth mindset can help you see the world as a place with endless possibilities. Without it, you might see the world as a place of lack and stop striving for a better life. You must believe that a better life is possible before you can find the motivation to make it happen.

Use the social skills you learned in Chapter 2 to keep up with your confidence in conversation, and simply: Rehearse, Relax, Rethink, Results, and Repeat.

CELEBRATIONS AND SETBACKS

Your recovery journey is not going to be a process of gradual improvement with no setbacks. I need you to be okay with that. Just like the winner of a race is not always at the front the entire time, eventually, they cross the finish line. That's all that matters.

Along your journey, you are your only competition. Sometimes you'll be the runner breaking the ribbon, and sometimes you'll be the one tripping and falling. The only time you should see setbacks as a failure is if you give up. I need you to make a promise to yourself that when you fall, you're going to get up and keep trying. Again, as long as you're making progress, you're winning.

I understand that giving up can sometimes feel like the only choice. There is a reason for that. It's not because your setbacks are too big, but rather that you are not giving yourself the recognition and encouragement you need to continue. Celebrating your wins, no matter how small, is the key to staying motivated.

Let me repeat that: Celebration is the key to motivation.

With all the highs and lows that come with life, your perseverance is worth your acknowledgment. You need to find ways to make a big fuss over the progress you're making.

Take a moment, right now, to share one win you've accomplished in the LearnWell Community, and let us all celebrate with you!

Don't let anybody tell you that the effort you're making isn't enough. As long as you're moving forward and making positive changes, recognize your success.

If you're not feeling supported with your journey, I need you to stop relying on the validation and approval of others. While a great support system is extremely valuable, recovery is a very personal journey that can be difficult for others to understand. You need to focus on giving yourself the validation and approval you need. It is a great reward to give yourself for your progress.

Celebration is the key to motivation.

You know yourself better than anyone. Try to think about the meaningful ways that you can show yourself appreciation. You're facing this journey for yourself. It is a valiant thing to do. Ensure you feel a sense of accomplishment each time you achieve a goal or overcome a challenge. Even if you've had to start back at Chapter 1 of the first book, you were brave enough not to give up.

It can be defeating to feel like you've failed. But by now, you should be more comfortable with failure and able to move on with self-love and compassion. Success is not about constant progress, it is rather about how fast you can return from failure and keep moving forward. Be realistic about setbacks, and be prepared to catch yourself when you fall.

How you handle setbacks and failures can also affect your motivation to continue. That's where having the right strategies to make a comeback is essential. Whether you're enjoying a peak or enduring a valley, I want you to make self-care a substantial part of your long-term healing strategy.

YOUR LONG-TERM SELF-CARE PLAN

As you now know, there is a chain of command for healing social anxiety. It goes like this:

- Acknowledging the problem is social anxiety
- Transforming your thoughts to heal false beliefs
- Breaking the pattern of self-doubt with self-confidence
- Reducing your anxiety with relaxation techniques

- Improving your social skills to help you succeed
- Breaking the avoidance cycle
- Gradually exposing yourself to fears in a fun way
- Addressing and healing the root patterns behind your greatest fears
- Staying on track socially and managing setbacks

These are the main goals of each chapter throughout these books. While it is a lot to cover and remember, there is one thing that is universal across each step: Self-love.

Self-love is going to allow you to maintain a life without social anxiety. It is what allows you to have the confidence to trip in front of a group of people and genuinely laugh at yourself. When you love yourself fully and wholeheartedly, no one can bring you down – at least not for long.

I know that you already love yourself to some degree. You wouldn't have bothered reading these books if you didn't. Without self-love, you wouldn't have made it through every exercise, strategy, or outcome. But the kind of self-love that can defeat the tsunami wave of social anxiety is one that takes practice and persistence. It requires reminding yourself of this love and reinforcing everything you do with it.

You have already learned a lot about self-love, self-care, and compassion by now. But I want you to put everything you've learned, plus a few extra strategies, into one long-term self-care plan. Self-care is often interchangeable with self-love, but for the sake of this plan, your self-care strategies are *how* you will build an unbreakable self-love.

A great self-care plan looks like this:

- **Journaling:** A minimum of 15 minutes of journaling before bed. Focus on working through struggles, writing down my thoughts, or just writing about my day.

- **Mindfulness meditation:** Practice deep breathing and mindfulness with morning coffee/tea.

- **Relaxation techniques:** Practice the 5-Step Solution To Solve Fight-Or-Flight when anxious.

- **Practicing gratitude:** Write down 5 things I'm grateful for from the day every evening.

- **Regular exercise:** Move my body for at least 30 minutes a day doing something I enjoy.

- **Time in nature:** Make sure I spend time outdoors without technology, even if it's just 15 minutes on the lawn every day or an outing once a week.

- **Positive media use:** Stick to consuming media that has a positive influence on my life. For example, listening to uplifting music, watching funny movies, reading self-help books, or following inspirational social media accounts.

- **Rest and repair:** Spend time daily doing something unrelated to work or accomplishing anything. Do things that activate my rest-and-repair response, like taking a hot bath with candles, playing a fun game, quality time with

- **Positive affirmations:** Repeat my chosen "I am" statements in the mirror before bed to help me improve my confidence and release any other doubts or insecurities I have.

- **Manage my energy:** Stay in tune with my social battery and make sure I stick to my boundaries, even if that means saying "no" to plans out of self-care.

This is only an example of what your long-term self-care plan should look like. I want you to use this plan as a reference to write your own. Feel free to use any of the strategies I've written in this example, but don't be afraid to add some of your own.

The reason you need to write out a plan for yourself is because you're unique. Everyone experiences and recognizes love in a different way. I need your long-term self-care plan to be tailored to your needs. You can use any strategy or activity from this book, or add some of your own. Go to your Workbook now and find your blank Long-Term Self-Care Plan waiting for you.

BUILDING SOCIAL SUPPORT

One last cog I need to address in your anti-anxiety system is your level of social support. Don't overlook the power of maintaining healthy relationships and having positive social experiences. These two things are a great way to reinforce everything you've worked so hard to achieve.

If you are around the wrong people all of the time, you're setting yourself up for endless setbacks on your recovery journey. Even though it was my symptoms of anxiety that caused my friends to call me a "buzzkill" that time I wouldn't go out with them, they certainly didn't add to my comfort. The wrong friends or relationships can hinder your progress and give you more to be anxious about.

For example, if someone is in an abusive relationship, you wouldn't say that they are socially anxious around their partner. Their anxiety is warranted by the repeated negative experiences they have around that person. Make sure you surround yourself with people who love you, support your journey, and do their best to make you feel comfortable around them.

People with empathy and compassion will naturally draw you in and make you feel like you can be yourself around them. They won't reject you for being socially anxious unless your anxiety is getting in the way of you reciprocating the friendship – even then, a good friend will reach out first rather than jumping to conclusions.

Good company makes reciprocation easier. Focus on how you feel around the people you're with and try to limit your friendships to genuine connections instead of surface-level relationships.

Genuine friendships can look like:

- Enthusiasm to spend time with you
- Two-way conversations rather than a sense of selfishness
- Friends that text you first

- A desire to get to know you
- Feeling relaxed together
- Silences that don't feel awkward
- Respect for your boundaries and needs
- A willingness to listen and understand your perspective during conflict
- Conversations run deeper than surface-level topics
- No offense taken if you decline plans out of self-care

Once you have built up your confidence and find people you can trust with your vulnerability, don't stay cooped up alone. Go out, be around great friends, and have the most fun you've ever had in your life. Laugh, dance, play. Let go of fear, and embrace your social self with open arms.

But don't stop there.

Now that you're ahead of the game, share your success with others. Use your tools and newfound confidence to encourage your shy friends to come out and have fun with you. Share the joy you've been able to find, and let everyone willing to listen in on your secrets. After all, there's no better way to learn for yourself than to teach.

When you're ready, turn the page for a final check-in and goodbye. You've made it to the end of these books and you deserve my appreciation. See you there.

IN 90 SECONDS YOU CAN MAKE A HUGE DIFFERENCE

If you feel we've deserved it, please take a moment to leave a review on Amazon.

Your feedback means the world to us. It helps us to improve and it means better learning experiences for all our readers.

We'd be so grateful to you for your review!

Thank you!
Thank you!
Thank you! ♥

CONCLUSION

You've done it. You took a chance at discovering and experiencing the life you deserve. You're here and it's beautiful. Maybe it's not perfect, but it's yours and you worked so hard for it. The grips of social anxiety have weakened off of you. You're free.

I know it's been a challenge, and your journey is ongoing. But I want you to take a moment to be unwaveringly proud of yourself. I'm so proud of you for making it through. The life you've envisioned – the one with the laughter, the memories, and the joy – **is yours.**

Now take a moment to reflect on the first time you opened the first book. Think about where you were, why you were there, and how you were feeling. Maybe your shoulders were hunched, your eyes were tired, and you felt desperate to catch a break. Something brought you here.

When I asked you whether or not you were brave at the beginning of Book 1, what did you answer? Whatever it was, I'm sure your voice quivered as you spoke, and your pulse quickened. How about now? Are you brave?

Yes. You are.

At the start of this journey, I warned you that it was going to be tough, but you turned the page anyway. When you were confronted with your anxiety experience, you stood up and faced it. You put in the work to prepare yourself and heal, even when what you saw was ugly. Then, when I asked you to go out into the world and actively do the scary things you've been too anxious to do, you had fun with it. Only true bravery can find fun in fear.

Now take that bravery and continue to find the fun in places where anxiety tells you there's only fear. Take the confidence you've built and show people that you're exactly where you need to be.

But this time, you're not cooped up in the dark searching for answers. You're out in the world lighting up every room you enter. Don't be afraid to shine – you'd be surprised who needs a beacon.

REFERENCES

1. https://www.nimh.nih.gov/health/statistics/social-anxiety-disorder#:~:text=An%20estimated%2012.1%25%20of%20U.S.,some%20time%20in%20their%20lives.
2. https://pubmed.ncbi.nlm.nih.gov/30877413/
3. https://www.ncbi.nlm.nih.gov/books/NBK519712/table/ch3.t12/
4. https://online.utpb.edu/about-us/articles/communication/how-much-of-communication-is-nonverbal/#:~:text=It%20was%20Albert%20Mehrabian%2C%20a,%2C%20and%207%25%20words%20only.
5. https://ourworldindata.org/optimism-and-pessimism
6. https://www.ncbi.nlm.nih.gov/pmc/articles/PMC4814782/
7. https://www.researchgate.net/publication/281147043_Neuroscience_and_advertising_Redefining_the_role_of_the_unconscious

www.ingramcontent.com/pod-product-compliance
Lightning Source LLC
Chambersburg PA
CBHW020409080526
44584CB00014B/1238